The Banana Wars

A Captivating Guide to the Interventions of the United States in Central America, Mexico, and the Caribbean

Free Bonus from Captivating History (Available for a Limited time)

Hi History Lovers!

Now you have a chance to join our exclusive history list so you can get your first history ebook for free as well as discounts and a potential to get more history books for free! Simply visit the link below to join.

Captivatinghistory.com/ebook

Also, make sure to follow us on Facebook, Twitter and Youtube by searching for Captivating History.

Table of Contents

Introduction

The Banana Wars were a series of American military and political interventions in Central America, the Caribbean, and Mexico. They took place between the end of the Spanish-American War in 1898 and the announcement of the Good Neighbor Policy in 1934 by Franklin Roosevelt's administration. One factor involved in these wars was, obviously, bananas. The region had plenty of semitropical lowlands conducive to the crop, and those bananas offered potentially highly profitable opportunities to American entrepreneurs.

A second set of factors were geopolitical. The United States had expanded to the Pacific and had become a major maritime power; it was concerned about potential rivals, identified at the time as Japan in the Pacific and Germany in the Atlantic. Geography made Central America of great interest to the United States because there were several possible routes for a transoceanic canal—Mexico's Isthmus of Tehuantepec, through Nicaragua via rivers and Lake Nicaragua, and across Panama. Crossing Panama to get to the Pacific became important after gold was discovered in California in 1848. Taking a ship from New Orleans to Panama, crossing it, and taking a ship from Panama City to California was the fastest way there until the transcontinental railroad was completed in 1869. A canal would also make it easy to shift battleships from one ocean to the other. The Caribbean became important as the approach to the canal once it was built, which meant Cuba and Hispaniola (the island Haiti and the Dominican Republic share) became strategic.

A third factor is that the countries, except Mexico and Colombia, were relatively small and weak and could be easily bossed around. Americans did not completely dominate the hemisphere but came close.

The interventions earned the name "Bananas Wars" because several American companies, most particularly the United Fruit Company, habitually called on Washington whenever the companies felt that local governments were becoming unfriendly, labor was getting restive, or political violence threatened American lives or property.

Several technologies had to come together before the international banana trade became profitable. In bunches, bananas are heavy and bulky, so getting them to shipping points required that railroads be built. Bananas are perishable, so fast and reliable steamers were needed to get them to market, and refrigeration made shipping masses of bananas feasible. Then, the banana companies had to convince a public living in temperate zones, where traditional fruits were apples, pears, and peaches, that a tropical fruit was worth buying. The companies solved this with highly successful campaigns emphasizing that bananas were healthy, tasty, and cheap.

The last factor was the impact of individual personalities interacting with the circumstances of their time and place. Among the personalities were Augusto Sandino, a barely five-foot-tall Nicaraguan rebel whom the Marines could never run to ground, and a Dominican dictator who invited a rival to a dinner in the presidential palace. Then there's Francisco Madero, a frail intellectual Mexican President who overturned a dictator. A vegetarian, teetotaler, and spiritualist, Madero was murdered in a coup d'état led by a crude soldier named Victoriano Huerta, who later colluded with the Germans to keep the US out of World War 1.

The cast also included Samuel Zemurray, an immigrant from Bessarabia who was introduced to bananas by working as a longshoreman on the docks of Mobile, Alabama, unloading them from ships. He built up a rival to United Fruit in Honduras, gaining concessions from a man he helped become president by hiring thugs and mercenaries. Another memorable cast member was the swashbuckling Major General Smedley Butler, a lifetime US Marine who fought in China, the Philippines, Mexico, Nicaragua, and elsewhere. After he retired, Butler wrote a book and gave a memorable speech on how his career was comparable to being a gangster for bankers and fruit companies.

The US occupied Cuba four times and Nicaragua, Haiti, and the Dominican Republic for years. The military occupations built schools, bridges, and roads, made a major dent in the prevalence of diseases, and killed thousands of rebels.

The story of the Banana Wars is an entertaining and sometimes tragic history, but it helps to make sense of the present and how the nations of the region regard the United States.

Chapter 1: Bananas and the Banana Wars

American interventions in Latin America were common long before the Banana War era. American forces (usually Navy personnel or Marines) landed in Argentina in 1833, 1852, and 1890; in Peru in 1835; in Nicaragua in 1853, 1853, 1854, 1896, and 1899; in Uruguay 1855, 1858, and 1868; in Mexico (aside from the Mexican War) in 1870; in Chile in 1891; in Panama 1860, 1875, 1885, and 1895, and this is an incomplete list (Boot 60).

That the United States has such an extensive history of interventions and small wars with a global reach is not well known. Americans fought their first foreign wars in North Africa in the early 1800s and repeatedly tried to invade Canada during the American Revolution and the War of 1812. American naval force was used in Sumatra in 1832 and 1839, in China in 1854, 1856, and 1900, in Japan in 1864, in a bloody incident in Korea in 1871, and in Hawaii and Samoa in 1889. A US Navy ship fought in the Marquesas Islands as early as 1813, and naval detachments disputed the Falkland Islands with Argentina in 1831 and landed in Egypt in 1882. Again, this is an incomplete list (Boot 60).

A major element of the Banana Wars interventions was the US Marine Corps. The Corps went back to the Revolution. All navies had aboard what was sometimes called naval infantry. Marines served as the police force aboard ships, protecting the officers. In the Royal Navy, the crews were often press-ganged into service (a kind of draft) and sometimes recruited from jails. The Royal Marines were a guard against mutiny, and the American Marines served the same way, although the crews were better paid and volunteers.

Marines also provided force when warships were in foreign ports. They might be called in to protect the lives of their nationals or provide guards for embassies or the local consuls. They also traditionally provided an important function in combat: boarding the enemy ship and taking it over. That function vanished with the advent of more efficient cannons onboard warships, which could engage at a considerable distance. Marines still sometimes functioned as sharpshooters in combat and guards for a captured enemy.

The anthem of the US Marine Corps references past interventions. The Marine Hymn includes the line "From the halls of Montezuma to the shores of Tripoli." The "shores of Tripoli" refers to the First Barbary War, when in 1805, Marines were part of a land campaign against the Barbary pirate center at Tripoli, now in Libya. The "halls of Montezuma" refers to the Mexican War when Marines were involved in the battle to take over Mexico City in 1847, the climatic battle of the Mexican War.

The US Navy had squadrons in the Mediterranean and the Caribbean, near West Africa to help stop the slave trade (domestic American slavery was legal, but the international slave trade was not), in the South Atlantic off Brazil, and in Asia. A Navy flotilla commanded by Commodore Matthew Perry famously "opened" Japan in 1853. Also little known is that American warships cooperated with the Royal Navy many times in suppressing piracy in the Caribbean and near China and in suppressing the slave trade.

American interventions were common and global. What was new about the Banana Wars era interventions was the relationship between American corporations in the Caribbean and the government's readiness to send in the Marines on their request. The Banana Wars also contained three other elements: the pervasive theories of the highly influential American naval theorist Alfred Thayer Mahan, growing concerns about German naval adventurism, and the need for a canal allowing the US Navy to readily move battleships between the Atlantic and Pacific.

The term "banana republic" has an unusual history. It comes from a 1904 collection of short stories written by the once-famous American writer, O. Henry, the pseudonym of William Sydney Porter, who was in Honduras in 1896-97 (Piatti-Farnell 93). Where the term "banana wars" came from is unknown. It may have come from the Marine Corps, perhaps because some of the many interventions the Marines were involved in between 1898 and 1934 consisted of banana companies calling on Washington to send in troops. Or, it may be that the juxtaposition of the words "banana" and "war" made the term memorable.

The usual villain in the history of the Banana Wars is the United Fruit Company, which resulted from a merger in 1899. United Fruit quickly became so dominant in the banana industry that the antitrust sentiment of the US government forced it to sell off a subsidiary, Vaccaro Brothers Company. This became United Fruit's competitor and the precursor to Standard Fruit, later named Dole (Jansen).

United Fruit was not the only American corporation in the region that called on Washington for help (which might be diplomacy or sending in the Marines). Neither were fruit companies the only American businesses involved. American business activity in Central America and the Caribbean also included sugar plantations, gold mining, railroads, and shipping lines. Nor was a business calling in the military just an American phenomenon—the British, French, Germans, and others did the same.

United Fruit became dominant by forming a vertical monopoly and employing ruthless business tactics to destroy its competition. It also frequently used local governments to repress any labor strikes or attempts to unionize, not hesitating to use bribes or mercenaries or even subsidize a rebellion or coup d'état. The ultimate threat was to call in the Marines.

There are a thousand varieties of bananas, and they have been grown all over the world for many centuries. The remaining wild species of bananas are close to inedible and full of seeds. Bananas grow best in a semitropical climate between twenty and thirty degrees Celsius, making the Caribbean and Central American nations perfect for the crop.

Cultivated seedless bananas, which have almost completely dominated the trade for over a century, cannot be planted because they are all clones. In technical terms, they are *parthenocarpic*. Today's varieties have resulted from selective breeding centuries ago and, more recently, from genetic manipulation. They are planted by removing the shoots that grow from the base of a mature banana plant and planting them separately. Some of the hundreds of varieties of bananas do grow from seeds, but those varieties are of little use for more than local consumption. A banana plant is a perennial, and it grows back each year. A plant has a productive lifespan of about twenty to twenty-five years.

The fact that bananas are all clones makes them highly vulnerable to diseases because, if a fungus or pest mutates and finds bananas especially good as a host, all the bananas of that variety become vulnerable. If a banana plantation becomes infected, it is destroyed (Piatti-Farnell 24-25).

Bananas are closely related to plantains, which grow much like bananas but are cooked and treated more like vegetables than fruit. In formal terms, bananas are not fruit. They are berries, and the banana trees are not trees but very large herbs. However, bananas are almost universally called fruit. Bananas grow on a kind of stalk from the main stem of the plant and are called a bunch. A bunch will have several smaller groups of bananas with a common stem, called "hands," probably from their resemblance to human fingers (Piatti-Farnell 7).

Bananas reached the Americas from Spain's Canary Islands probably at some point in the middle 1500s. The Canaries have a sufficiently mild climate, so some tropical crops can be grown there. Bananas probably reached the Canaries from Spanish endeavors in West Africa. It is unclear how bananas spread in the islands and Central America, but they were connected with the slave trade because they were used as food in many African cultures. The closely-related plantain also reached the Americas that way. Bananas and plantains were staples during slavery times and remain part of regional cuisines.

During the Banana Wars era, most of the labor was performed by field hands who cut the bunches and then carried them to a collection point. They were cut by hand using a machete, and the work was hard. Laborers had to deal with not only the tropical heat and humidity but also stinging insects and venomous snakes. A deadly problem was the prevalence of tropical fevers. Workers often lived in squalid housing with no running water and minimal sanitation. Often the labor used on Central American plantations was imported from the West Indies, adding a complicating element of race and cultural difference.

Bananas as a large-scale commodity are a relatively modern phenomenon. They are heavy, prone to spoiling, and grow far from the major markets in North America and Europe. The first task was getting bananas to a port. Donkey carts or ox teams could not get bananas to a port quickly enough, but once railroads began to appear, they were quickly adopted, and large plantations often built narrow-gauge railways to carry the bunches to a port. The first development of rail in Central America was to connect the Caribbean coast and the Pacific side of the countries. The population in those days was heavily concentrated on the Pacific side, with the Caribbean lowlands being the haunt of malaria, yellow fever, various other diseases, stinging flies, caimans, and snakes.

Getting the bananas to a port by rail solved one problem but getting them to market was another problem. Sailing ships were simply too slow and unreliable to consistently carry the crop to market, even to relatively close ports such as New Orleans or Mobile, Alabama. The development of steamships from about 1850 on solved that problem. Yet another problem was spoilage; the ships were still in the tropics when they loaded and, depending on their speed, might lose the entire cargo to spoilage before reaching port. The solution emerged in the middle 1870s: refrigerated steamships. These spread widely by the 1880s and got fresh bananas to ports, just as they got Argentine beef and New Zealand lamb to Britain.

Shipping posed a geographic problem. A thousand-mile swath of the Central American Caribbean coast has few harbors, and that port-poor swath of coast happened to be prime territory for banana plantations. From Costa Rica to Belize, there are only five usable ports: Puerto Barrios in Guatemala, Porto Cortes and Trujillo in Honduras, Puerto Limon in Costa Rica, and the Boca del Toro in Panama. There were more ports to the south in Panama.

Steamships used in the banana trade were considerably larger than the sailing ships of the past, and having deeper drafts, they needed larger facilities and deeper water. In addition, the first steamers used could carry about 2,000 bunches, but by the 1880s, steamers carried 12,000 to 20,000 bunches (Abbott 3-4).

There was another issue for steamers: hazards at sea. The hurricane season lasts six months, and the growth cycle of bananas required that some be shipped during the half year when hurricanes could strike. Ships were now and then lost at sea. Hurricanes could also damage plantation and port infrastructure, destroy a crop, and sometimes cause heavy loss of life.

Railroads, steamships, and refrigeration made the banana trade possible. But there was yet another problem: labor. The Caribbean coastal lowlands that were such good lands for growing bananas were very lightly populated, and banana plantations needed large amounts of labor. That was partly solved by bringing in labor from the Caribbean islands, particularly Jamaica and other English-speaking islands, where jobs were scarce and labor plentiful. This created other problems because Jamaican laborers spoke English and were not Catholic. Jamaicans also tended to be restive because, while Jamaica was still a colony, thy were used to relatively egalitarian British rule, not the kind of regime American companies brought with them to the banana lands, which was thoroughly Jim Crow after the Civil War.

As if those weren't enough factors to worry about, another was keeping both managers and labor alive. The Caribbean lowlands were lightly populated for a reason: they were unhealthy. Annual epidemics of malaria and yellow fever were common, and diseases like typhus and cholera were occasional visitors. United Fruit and other companies built what in the United States would be called company towns and did their best to defeat mosquito-borne diseases. The realization that mosquitoes were disease vectors was new and largely the result of a theory of disease transmission developed by Carlos Finlay, a Cuban doctor, and the work of the American army doctor Walter Reed during the American occupation of Cuba. It was found that some diseases were transferred by mosquito bites, so mosquito control went a long way to cut down on disease fatalities.

In addition, a fungal disease appeared that is still fatal to bananas. Called Panama disease (where it was first noticed a century ago), it is highly communicable from soil, water, or even the hands and clothes of agriculture workers. During the era of the Banana Wars, United Fruit bought far more land than it needed for its banana plantations as a kind of insurance. When Panama disease infected a plantation, the only recourse was to destroy the banana trees and move to another area that was not yet infected. It was the custom for United Fruit to destroy not only a plantation where banana disease broke out but also the infrastructure used to harvest the crop so no competitor could take over the land and try growing again.

The predominant kind of banana grown during the banana wars is no longer available. It went extinct by 1960 from Panama disease. The variety was called the Gros Michel and differed from the contemporary banana marketed in North America, the Cavendish. The Gros Michel had thicker skin and was less susceptible to bruising and damage during the picking and transportation stages. It is also said to have had a creamier texture and a better taste than Cavendish (Piatti-Farnell 16-18).

The differences between today's dominant Cavendish variety and the once-dominant Gros Michel changed some production conditions. The

Cavendish was more delicate and required gentler handling. It had a higher yield of bananas per acre and could be grown indefinitely on the same land as long as Panama disease didn't strike. The Cavendish variety is considerably more labor intensive than the Gros Michel was (Jansen).

There's another factor that doesn't get much attention from historians: the entire banana trade depended on being able to sell bananas. Americans historically ate the fruit that could be grown at home in a temperate climate: numerous varieties of apples, pears, peaches, cherries, and berries where they were available. That brings up the question of how Americans were persuaded to buy a tropical fruit that was not traditionally consumed. It took a sustained advertising campaign over several years to grow the market to the point that large banana sales became possible. The main theme of the campaign was to convince the public that bananas were very healthy and that a banana a day would contribute to good health (Piatti-Farnell 45).

This may seem trivial, but if Americans and Europeans had not been convinced to buy bananas, there would have been no banana companies or banana republics. There would likely still have been American interventions for geopolitical reasons, such as the need for the Panama Canal. Still, there would have been no United Fruit calling on a country's army to break a strike or calling in the Marines to intimidate a local government.

Chapter 2: The United Fruit Company and the Banana Wars

Developing banana plantations large enough to be profitable was complicated, and to do it effectively required substantial capital. First, some kind of agreement had to be made with the local and national authorities about access to land, whether leasing or purchasing. Then came clearing the jungle or forests. A labor force had to be recruited for clearing the land, building the infrastructure, and planting, growing, and harvesting the crop. (As mentioned, in the later 1800s and early 1900s, the regions involved in banana production were the least populated areas of countries with low populations—most of the population in Central America was in the highlands and on the Pacific side of the mountains.)

Getting labor to bananas and bananas to shipping points required housing and transportation. That meant railroads to carry the bananas to ports, often narrow-gauge rail. It meant at least some port facilities to get bananas aboard steamers, and the steamers needed to be scheduled and routed. Shipping also meant insuring the ships and cargo and unloading and getting produce to markets. All this required supervision, contracts, quality control, managers, and security. And given the vulnerability of banana plantations to hurricanes and civil disturbance, having plantations in several different countries was good planning.

The venture's long-term success also depended on agreements with the heads of state involved in the highly volatile politics of the nations in the regions. One year, a president might be friendly to American companies;

the next year, the friendly president might be overturned in a coup, resulting in a dictator wanting a bigger share of the profits. Unrest often brought riots and wars that could destroy infrastructure and endanger workers and managers. It's understandable that the companies might appeal to Washington to send in the Marines or quietly fund a coup to eliminate an uncooperative president. The banana corporation that was the largest, most profitable, and perhaps most prone to request support from the Marines was, of course, United Fruit.

United Fruit is closely connected with a remarkable American entrepreneur named Minor Keith. Keith became involved in Central America because an uncle had been constructing railroads in Chile and Peru. His uncle realized that the young man had great potential and saw to it that Minor Keith was placed as a manager of the project to build a coast-to-coast railroad in Costa Rica. Keith was in his early twenties with little experience other than observing how his uncle did things.

Building the railroad was difficult because the terrain was rugged, disease rampant, and unrest common. The young man proved an excellent choice and got it done. Keith had to import labor, much of it from Jamaica. At the time, the swampy Caribbean lowlands of the country were disease-ridden, and building the Costa Rican Railroad cost about 4,000 lives (Abbott 8).

While building the Costa Rican railway, Minor Keith was alert to other possibilities. Bananas seemed to be an opportunity, and he took it. At first, he bought bananas from farmers in Panama and marketed them in New Orleans, shipping 250 to 400 bunches a month. This proved profitable enough that Keith bought land in Costa Rica and adjacent Panama. Over several years, he began to establish banana plantations in Costa Rica, Panama (which was still a province of Colombia), and the Magdalen department in Colombia. He based his company in New Orleans. He had the support of the Costa Rican government, so when a competitor, the American Banana Company, cleared land in Costa Rica for banana plantations, they were evicted by the Costa Rican army (Abbott 7).

Keith expanded into Colombia, which proved congenial for a time. Production in Colombia grew to 175,000 bunches in 1892 and then 1,170,000 by 1899. This was interrupted by the civil war called the Thousand Days' War, a bloody civil war between the Liberal and Conservative parties in which more than a hundred thousand lives were lost. The United States intervened in Panama to protect American property. It helped the two sides in Colombia negotiate a cease-fire, and the treaty ending the war was signed on the American battleship USS *Wisconsin.*

Keith married into an influential Costa Rican family, marrying the daughter of the country's chief justice, Dr. Jose Maria Castro, who was also a former president. By 1890, Keith was the largest banana producer in the world. Competition increased, and price wars emerged, threatening several competing companies. In 1899, Keith, apparently near bankruptcy, traveled to Boston and negotiated an advantageous merger for all concerned. The parties in the merger included Keith, who had banana plantations in Colombia and Costa Rica, railroad interests in Costa Rica, and dominated the banana market in the Southeast United States. The second major party in the merger was Preston and Baker, based in Boston, which owned a steamship line and dominated the banana market in the Northeast. Thus, the United Fruit Company was formed (Han).

The new company controlled 212,000 acres of good banana land in six countries, of which 38,000 acres were in production, with 112 miles of railroad. It owned or chartered a fleet of forty-four steamships. The company never had a monopoly, but it was the largest single banana producer, with a 70 percent share of the trade in 1900 (Abbott 11).

Colombia is a good example of how United Fruit and other companies squeezed profit from suppliers. In Colombia, an excellent region for setting up banana plantations was in the Magdalena section of the country—at that time, impoverished and sparsely populated. Bogota wanted development in the region but had few resources to work with, so it welcomed United Fruit. Local entrepreneurs had tried growing and exporting bananas as early as 1887, but the efforts failed because they lacked access to fast, refrigerated steamers. There was something of a rail network in the region, but more was needed. The Colombian government awarded concessions to United Fruit. Colombia was experiencing a period of peace following the bloody civil war, so the political climate was favorable (Bucheli 185).

United Fruit grew bananas on its own farms in Colombia but also relied on purchasing bananas from independent producers. It was from these independent producers that the company obtained a large portion of its bananas, and the required contracts were written to the company's advantage. Contracts placed most of the risks on the producers and assigned most of the profit to the company. The suppliers were required to sell bananas only to United Fruit, but the company was not obligated to buy the crop. The contracts specified that the bananas became the property of United Fruit as soon as they were cut from the tree. But, if the company discovered defects, ownership automatically reverted to the producers. If the bananas were rejected by US agricultural inspectors when the fruit reached American ports, ownership reverted to the producers, and they received no payment (Bucheli 189).

The company could reject any bananas for any reason, and the producer would not be paid. Yet, growing bananas was one of the few ways Colombians in the region could make money, so they agreed to United Fruit's terms. They accepted the contracts because, if they wanted to grow bananas to export, there was only one choice. Beginning a banana operation required financing. United Fruit was willing to provide loans on the condition all the produce be sold to the company. There were no Colombian banks or financial services in the region, so the company did provide an important service for local people, even with the conditions attached.

United Fruit used another technique with the contracts made with local producers. The expiration dates were staggered so that only a few expired at a time. This prevented competitors or local entrepreneurs from contracting with suppliers in any significant numbers at a time. The company also had very good lawyers who could manipulate the courts. For example, in 1920, some Colombian producers made a deal with the Atlantic Fruit Company, based in New Orleans. When the first shipment got to New York in September 1920, it was seized by New York customs when United Fruit complained that the shipment violated a contract. Seized fruit would not last long, which was the object (Bucheli 191).

The most infamous incident of the entire Banana War era did not involve an American intervention; it involved an action designed to prevent United Fruit from calling in the Marines. The incident occurred in Ciénaga, Colombia, on December 6, 1928. United Fruit had sizable banana plantations in that area, dating back to Minor Keith's banana production in Colombia a generation before. On December 1, workers at the United Fruit plantations went on strike, demanding an eight-hour day and six-day work week and that their pay be in cash rather than coupons for food.

United Fruit called on the Colombian government to do something about the strike. It is not known if the company threatened to have

Washington send in the Marines, but the government acted to end the strike and eliminate the need for American military intervention. Units of the Colombian army under General Cortes Vargas reached Ciénaga in early December. On December 5, 1928, the town square filled up with strikers and the strikers' wives and children. The army surrounded the square with troops and placed machine guns on the roofs of nearby buildings. The strikers refused to disperse, so the general ordered the troops to fire on the unarmed crowds. The result was slaughter. General Cortes Vargas admitted that forty-seven people were killed, but estimates are that as many as 2,000 to 3,000 people were killed. In Spanish, the massacre is called the *masacre de las bananeras*. It broke the strike, and no Marines were called in.

The bloody incident appears in the world-famous 1967 novel *One Hundred Years of Solitude* by the Colombian writer Gabriel Garcia Marquez, which has fixed the massacre and United Fruit in world consciousness. In the novel, the events are thinly disguised, but everyone knows the reference. Another earlier novel published by the American writer Gore Vidal in 1950 featured in its plot an American banana company supporting a coup d'état. The two novels did much to cement the idea of piratical and imperialistic American banana corporations making profits by manipulating violence and cruelly exploiting laborers (Piatti-Farnell 82, 95-97).

Following the horrendous event, United Fruit's dominance diminished in the country. Competitors entered the banana market, and several Colombian-owned banana companies emerged. United Fruit remained an important element in Colombia for years but gradually divested itself of its assets in Colombia.

United Fruit's most dangerous competitor was the Cuyamel Fruit Company, based in Honduras and headed by a remarkably able American entrepreneur named Samuel Zemurray. He was a charismatic and ruthless businessman—as ruthless as United Fruit—but seems to have been more innovative. Zemurray and his family migrated from Russian Bessarabia to New York, and he ended up working as a stevedore (longshoreman) in Mobile, Alabama. He became interested in bananas while unloading them from ships at the port and began marketing overripe bananas, buying them cheaply, and selling them to stores inland. Interested in the possibility of producing bananas himself, he traveled to Honduras. Liking what he saw, he founded his company in 1903, named after the Cuyamel River.

Zemurray took over a failing steamship company in 1905, and by 1910, Cuyamel had become a major banana producer. He was just as prone to interfering in local politics as United Fruit was. When government policies changed and he stood to lose a lot of money, Zemurray organized a mercenary force that managed to place a former president, Manuel Bonilla, back in office. A grateful Bonilla gave Cuyamel significant concessions and made sure United Fruit was only a minor presence in the country (Abbott 17).

Under Zemurray, Cuyamel led the industry in innovation. He developed better irrigation and pest control and engaged in agricultural research. Unlike most other Americans in the trade, he learned Spanish, and his workers were better treated. He also hired gun-toting mercenaries such as Lee Christmas and did not hesitate to use them to help friendly politicians and intimidate unfriendly ones.

In the late 1920s, Cuyamel and United engaged in an intense price and marketing war that threatened the profitability of both. In 1929, United offered Zemurray a deal, which he accepted. Zemurray sold his company to United Fruit for 300,000 shares of United stock. Not much later, he was named president of the merged company (Bucheli 192).

Chapter 3: Geopolitics and the Banana Wars

Several nations in Central America were involved in the Banana Wars. Four of them most often appear in accounts of the American interventions in the region: Costa Rica, Guatemala, Honduras, and Nicaragua. Two others were involved in different ways: British Honduras and Panama. Britain had a hazy authority over the Mosquito Coast region that became Belize, which meant British rule prevented American military intervention. Panama effectively became an American protectorate when it ceded the Panama Canal Zone to the US in 1903. The Caribbean islands of Cuba and Hispaniola (the island divided between Haiti and the Dominican Republic) were also frequently the sites of American interventions, partly because they were strategic to the approaches to Panama.

Despite looking small on a map, Central America is sizable—slightly more than 200,000 square miles. The largest of the countries is Nicaragua at 50,000 square miles, the size of New York. Guatemala and Honduras are roughly the same size at 43,000 and 42,000 square miles, about the size of Kentucky. Panama's 30,000 square miles is the size of South Carolina, and Costa Rica's 18,000 square miles is somewhat larger than Maryland. El Salvador's 8,000 square miles make it slightly larger than Hawaii. Except for El Salvador, each Central American nation has both Atlantic and Pacific coasts. The geography is varied, with rough mountains. At that time, there were large areas of jungle, swampy

Caribbean lowlands, mangrove swamps, and highlands on the Pacific side. Some popular assumptions about the geography of Central America are wrong. For example, the Panama Canal does not run east-west but closer to north-south as it connects the Pacific and Atlantic.

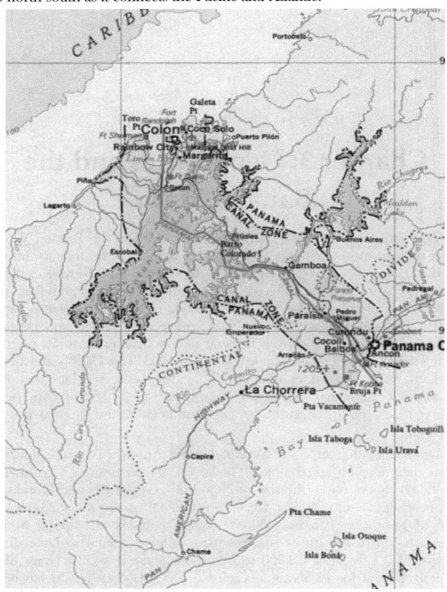

A 1970s map of the Panama Canal Zone.
https://en.wikipedia.org/wiki/File:CanalZone.png

All of these places were of interest to the United States for strategic reasons and their ability to grow vast quantities of bananas. But bananas were only part of the equation. A glance at a map of Central America and the Caribbean quickly shows why American interest in the region was so strong. Central America is shaped something like a twisted V, which at the bottom, tapers to a narrow isthmus in Panama. This immediately suggested that a canal could connect the Atlantic and Pacific. There were other possibilities for a canal, but Panama seemed superior.

That narrow isthmus became of surpassing interest to the United States when it acquired California in 1848 from the cessions forced on Mexico at the end of the Mexican War. The 1849 Gold Rush in California resulted in California becoming rapidly populated with immigrants, and it became a state in 1850. The overland route from Missouri, a common starting point, to the Pacific coast was by wagon or coach and took months. Whatever railroad and steamboat connections existed in the West ended at St. Louis. It was a long and sometimes dangerous trip to the Pacific coast. Sailing to California via Cape Horn was very nearly a circumnavigation of South America and took months. Taking a ship from New Orleans to Panama, crossing over, and then traveling by ship to California was much faster and less dangerous. The principal danger of the Panama route was disease rather than shipwreck or hostile Plains Indians.

Interest in a canal persisted even after the first transcontinental American railroad was completed in 1869. Railways cut the travel time to California from months to days, but even so, it was cheaper to ship goods by sea, so a canal would assist commerce. And there was another factor: getting warships to the West Coast. The US Navy had individual warships and sometimes a squadron in the Pacific and Asia from the 1820s on, and American trade with China dated to the 1780s. Sailing to Asia from the US meant going by way of Cape Horn or the Cape of Good Hope at the southern extremity of Africa. Although from early on several places on the West Coast were developed as naval bases, getting naval vessels to protect California meant the Cape Horn route.

The nations that experienced American intervention during the Banana Wars era were almost all Spanish-speaking Catholics and had gained independence from Spain between 1810 and 1824. There were some exceptions. Jamaica and the Mosquito Coast (now Belize) were British colonies, nominally Protestant, and spoke dialects of English. Haiti became independent from France in 1804 after an extraordinarily savage rebellion, and the Dominican Republic had to win independence from Spain in 1824, again in 1844 from Haiti, and again from Spain in 1865. Cuba remained a Spanish colony until 1898.

An important political aspect influenced US policy towards these nations. In 1823, President James Monroe promulgated the Monroe Doctrine. It stipulated that the United States would not tolerate any new attempts at European colonization in the Americas, Americans would not interfere with existing colonies, and the US would not interfere in Europe. In 1823, the US was a minor power. And, while it had considerable naval strength for its size, it is unlikely the Americans had the military ability to keep Europe away from the Americas. What made the policy work was that the Doctrine coincided with British interests. Britain had decided that the Americas were no longer a region for new colonies. British business interests predominated in South America, so keeping out potential competitors (such as the French) benefited British commerce. Britain retained several colonies, including Jamaica, Guyana, several smaller islands, and the Mosquito Coast.

The US population grew to more than thirty million people by 1860. And, at the end of the Civil War, it had the second-largest navy on the planet, behind only the Royal Navy. That huge naval force had been used to blockade the Confederacy and to hunt Confederate commerce raiders. When the war ended, the huge fleet was rapidly decommissioned, and American naval power almost vanished, falling well behind that of Chile and Brazil. By 1890, the US population had grown to sixty million, and the American economy had grown as large as Britain's. From about 1890, persistent and effective lobbying for a strong navy was led by the extremely influential American naval theorist Admiral Alfred Thayer Mahan and an increasingly influential politician with a very strong interest in the US Navy— Theodore Roosevelt.

In 1915, the total population of the Americas was about 185 million people, 102 million of which were in the United States. The US had more than half the total population of the American continents and probably closer to 85 percent of the total economic activity. The countries affected by American interventions in the Banana Wars era were, in relative terms, far weaker than today. In 1914, Guatemala had about 2 million people, El Salvador 1.2 million, Nicaragua 700,000, Panama 400,000, Honduras 500,000, and Costa Rica 400,000 (Jefferson 404).

The islands were also characterized by small populations: in 1914, Jamaica had 900,000, Cuba 2.5 million, the Dominican Republic 800,000, and Haiti perhaps 2 million. The larger nations affected by the interventions still had relatively low populations: Colombia had 4.4 million and Mexico 16 million (Jefferson 404).

A minor element in all this is that the US Marine Corps was nearly dissolved in the early 1900s. There was rivalry between the Navy and the Army, and many members of a parsimonious Congress saw no reason for a separate Marine Corps. During the Banana Wars, the Corps proved its usefulness as a fast-response intervention force and its ability to be a kind of constabulary, which contributed a great deal to its survival. Without the Banana Wars, the Marine Corps might have ceased to exist (Folse).

The Marines were especially useful in interventions. They were trained for small unit actions and could rapidly create ad hoc formations. Marines were stationed on warships on patrol and at US Navy bases. After construction of the Panama Canal began, Marines stationed in the Canal Zone were ready at hand. The Marines also established a base at Guantanamo in Cuba in 1903 as part of an agreement forced on the Cubans. Marines were traditionally assigned as guards at American embassies, and sometimes the number assigned was enough for action. The US Army was also used in the Banana Wars, but generally as a longer-term occupying force rather than a fast-reaction strike force. American military governors of occupied nations might be either Navy admirals or Army generals.

A look at the base at Guantanamo Bay in 1916.

In comparison, the armies of the Caribbean and Central American nations tended to be small and poorly trained. Recruits were often motivated to join because of their poverty. With army discipline at least came regular meals and (sometimes) pay. They were armed with an assortment of weapons, often surplus from wars fought elsewhere, such as the American Civil War or the wars in Cuba. Some forces had a limited number of machine guns, usually older models. Sometimes soldiers had machetes as weapons. They had a little artillery, and oddly, the Krupp weapons firm in Germany had a corner on artillery sales to El Salvador, Nicaragua, and Guatemala (Jowett 7).

Mexico had a good military academy and a naval academy, and officers in several Central American countries were schooled in military academies elsewhere. The armies and the rebels (and sometimes the rebels were the army) could fight with determination and courage, but facing a well-trained and well-armed professional military force like the US Marines was difficult and often fatal.

Another significant factor in the Banana Wars dovetailed with the Monroe Doctrine and resulted from a crisis in Venezuela. The country had taken out large loans from several European banks, and in 1902, President Cipriano Castro refused to make payments on the loans. This led to the Germans proposing to the British and the Italians that they take joint action to force Venezuela to pay. The three powers decided that a naval blockade of Venezuela would force payment. In early December 1902, they set up a blockade with warships from all three nations.

Just how the Monroe Doctrine was supposed to work in a blockade situation was unclear. The three powers were not interested in taking land from the Venezuelans, and no invasion was attempted. The blockade was maintained for more than a month. There was some fighting, with the British sinking several Venezuelan gunboats. At one point, British and German warships shelled the fort at Puerto Cabello after the fort had fired on the blockaders.

The United States was concerned about foreign warships in the Caribbean, especially those of the Germans. President Roosevelt had been an assistant secretary of the US Navy and was an advocate of Admiral Mahan's theories of how to use a navy. He had famously fought in Cuba in the war with Spain in 1898. By 1903 and the Venezuela Crisis, the US Navy had become a force to be reckoned with, well behind Britain's naval strength but not so far behind Germany's. Roosevelt had most of the US

Atlantic Fleet ordered to the Caribbean, ostensibly on maneuvers. It included about fifty warships under the command of Admiral Dewey, who had led the American Asian squadron to victory at the battle of Manila Bay in 1898. The three allies pulled their blockading ships out of the zone and agreed to arbitration.

In reaction to the 1903 crisis in Venezuela, President Teddy Roosevelt issued what has since become known as the Roosevelt Corollary in 1904. In effect, it amended the Monroe Doctrine by announcing that the United States reserved the right to intervene in any American nation when it acted inappropriately. The Corollary warned European intervention away, but it essentially said the US would intervene for them in matters of debt and threats to nationals or property. The Corollary was the political rationale that allowed the US to send the Marines into the Banana Wars.

Roosevelt's intent was to keep European intervention out of the Americas. However, he agreed that there was a need for occasional interventions to secure payment of loans, protect foreign nationals in times of disturbance, and preserve law and order. Under Roosevelt's Corollary, American forces became a kind of police force patrolling Central and South America.

Roosevelt wrote, "Chronic wrongdoing, or an impotence which results in a general loosening of the ties of civilized society, may, in America as elsewhere ultimately require intervention by some civilized nation." Roosevelt's reference to "some civilized nation" meant the United States. Roosevelt wrote that this civilized nation would exercise "an international police power," which included forcing payments for debts owed to American or European bankers (Boot 130).

The sentiment was not just Roosevelt's. In 1907, a professor named Woodrow Wilson, who would soon be president, wrote, "Concessions obtained by financiers must be safeguarded by ministers of state, even if the sovereignty of unwilling nations be outraged in the process" (Peace).

Photograph of President Woodrow Wilson.
https://commons.wikimedia.org/wiki/File:Thomas_Woodrow_Wilson,_Harris_%26_Ewing_bw_p hoto_portrait,_1919_(cropped).jpg

The nations involved had no say in how the Americans regarded them. The educated elites of these nations considered themselves civilized and often considered the United States to have a crass and overly materialistic culture. Nevertheless, the countries involved all experienced periods of domestic unrest and civil war and called on the United States to intervene. In many cases, American diplomats were sent in and managed to broker settlements.

There was some reason for concern about Germany as a possible intruder into the region. The Germans did, in fact, have a war plan to seize Cuba or Puerto Rico as a staging area for an attack on the United States. Called Operation Plan III, it was put aside in 1906. Whether this plan was serious or just an academic kind of war game is not clear. However, by then, the US had twenty battleships—as many as Germany—

and the success of the German plan would have been problematic (Boot 135). Early in the century, the American military had also considered the possibility of a German attack. Many thought a German attack would first seize Culebra, a small island off the east coast of Puerto Rico, and use it as a base for further attacks. Others thought a German attack would be aimed at the Chesapeake Bay region (Langley 14).

Chapter 4: The Banana Wars in Mexico

Mexico was not much involved in the banana trade, although the country had considerable lowland tropical areas that could grow the fruit. Neither was United Fruit involved in Mexico. Yet one of the Banana Wars interventions involved the American occupation of the port city of Veracruz for almost a year.

Mexico underwent a prolonged and exceedingly bloody civil war from 1910 to 1921. Long-time dictator Porfirio Díaz, who had ruled Mexico from 1876 to 1910, stepped down in 1910 and was replaced in 1911 with an idealistic and politically naïve man named Francisco Madero. Madero was just over five feet tall, a vegetarian, a teetotaler, and a spiritualist—most unusual traits in a Mexican president—but he was extremely popular (Langley 73). In 1913, Madero was the victim of a coup, murdered by a general who was .a main factor in the violence in 1914 in Veracruz: Victoriano Huerta.

An image of Huerta.
https://commons.wikimedia.org/wiki/File:Victoriano_Huerta.(cropped).jpg

During the Mexican Revolution, fighting occurred between American troops and civilians and Mexican revolutionaries, regular troops, and civilians along the border between Mexico and the American Southwest. It has sometimes been called the Mexican Border War, with the most intense phase being the US expedition into Mexico in 1916 in search of the revolutionary *caudillo* Pancho Villa. In a bloody skirmish, Villa had raided the town of Columbus, New Mexico, and President Wilson got Congressional authorization to send an army expedition into Mexico. It was much larger than the other American interventions in the Caribbean and Central America at about 10,000 men, led by General Blackjack Pershing. Pershing got that nickname from commanding African American troops in the West, and the general would soon command the two-million-man American Expeditionary Force in Europe in the war with Germany.

Photograph of John "Blackjack" Pershing.

https://commons.wikimedia.org/wiki/File:General_John_Joseph_Pershing_head_on_shoulders.jpg

The reason Americans landed in Veracruz in 1914 and fought a sizable battle seems, in retrospect, remarkably trivial. The invasion began because an American admiral was miffed that Mexican authorities in Tampico did not fire a 21-gun salute. Tampico was a smaller port north of Veracruz with a rapidly expanding oil industry characterized by very large American and other foreign investments. Naval vessels from several nations were stationed at Tampico, alert for threats to their nations from the worsening Revolution.

On April 9, 1914, eight sailors from the USS *Dolphin,* a Navy gunboat anchored at Tampico, took a small boat ashore to fill some gasoline cans from a warehouse. At the time, the US Navy had several ships at Tampico to protect American interests in the oil boom town where many

Americans were living and many American-owned businesses were operating. The serious political background to the incident was that Mexican General Victoriano Huerta had just taken power in a coup, having murdered the saintly Madero. American President Woodrow Wilson strongly disliked Huerta and wanted him brought down in any way legally possible.

Those eight sailors were arrested by Mexican soldiers, apparently for being in an area where they were not authorized to be. The sailors were taken into custody (only briefly), interrogated, and then released by Mexican Colonel Ramon Hinojosa. The American commander of the warships at Tampico was Admiral Henry T. Mayo, commander of one of the divisions of the Atlantic Fleet and later commander of the Atlantic Fleet during the First World War. For some reason, Mayo felt that the United States had been insulted. The boat the sailors were in had a small American flag flying, and the admiral interpreted the arrest as an insult to the American flag (Naval History).

Mayo demanded an apology, and the Mexican army commander at Tampico, General Zaragoza, offered the requested apology. But Mayo wanted more than just an apology. The Admiral wanted a formal repudiation of the arrest and severe punishment of the officer responsible. That wasn't all; he wanted to fly the American flag on shore in a prominent spot and have the Mexicans fire a 21-gun salute, which the Americans would answer with their own 21-gun salute. General Zaragoza was unwilling to meet those conditions and counteroffered that the Americans and Mexicans fire a 21-gun salute simultaneously. Americans refused the offer (Naval History).

This is where Admiral Mayo's irritation at a perceived insult gets mixed in with President Wilson's dislike of the dictator Huerta. Wilson had slapped an arms embargo on Mexico, preventing Huerta's soldiers from obtaining new weapons and ammunition. And as fate would have it, a large German freighter, the *Ypiranga*, was soon due to land at Veracruz. Its cargo was a large shipment of weapons: more than 17,000 cases of arms, including 200 machine guns and 17 million rounds of ammunition, all intended for Huerta's army. President Wilson saw the Tampico incident as a means to get at Huerta. Wilson asked Congress for quick authorization to intervene in Veracruz by sending a detachment ashore to occupy the port's customhouse. Congress complied, and on April 21, American warships arrived at Veracruz harbor and began sending troops ashore—Marines and sailors (Naval History).

The US Navy force at Veracruz was quite powerful. The force included several of the new dreadnought battleships (the kind the Germans and British used at the epic Battle of Jutland) and several pre-dreadnought battleships—seven or eight battleships in all—as well as other smaller warships. Admirals Mayo and Fletcher had the Tampico squadron that steamed to Veracruz reinforced by warships from Puerto Rico and other bases. On the morning of April 21, 1914, 787 officers and men landed, including 500 Marines. That number proved to be insufficient, so more troops were poured in.

The commander of the Mexican forces in the city of 40,000 was General Gustavo Maas. The Navy asked the general to cooperate and not resist the landing. Maas telegraphed Mexico City to ask what he should do because he had only a hundred soldiers. Huerta is said to have wired back that Maas should withdraw, but the message never got through. So, Maas passed out rifles to citizens, freed prisoners from the military and city jails, and armed them to fight the invaders (Naval History).

The landing forces quickly seized the docks, the railroad depot, the telegraph station, and other public buildings. The invading force came under sniper fire from many directions and responded by setting machine guns on the roofs of several buildings to provide cover fire. Marines started a systematic conquest of the city, block by block. The first contingent ran into unexpectedly fierce resistance and stalled. More Marines were poured in, a total of 3,000 reinforcements by the next day (Boot 153).

Some of the fire came from the Mexican Navy Academy, close to the harbor. Several warships in the harbor then blasted away at the academy buildings. The cadets were young, and the situation was eerily similar to an episode in the battle for Mexico City in the previous century when some young military cadets at Chapultepec fought hard, dying in defense of Mexico City and becoming Mexican heroes. At Veracruz, fifteen young naval cadets died in the battle, adding to that list of patriotic young Mexican heroes.

At the end of the first day, there were 4,000 Americans ashore, a combination of sailors and Marines. American losses on the first day were four killed and twenty-two wounded. The next day, the troops were formed into three regiments. The Marine regiment ran into heavy fire, so instead of advancing down the streets, they cleared the opposition house to house by breaking through adobe wall after adobe wall and clearing out snipers house by house. It was likely the hardest fighting in any of the Banana Wars interventions. The fighting ended after a second day of firefights.

In the middle of all this, the *Ypiranga* appeared. The German captain refused to land his cargo in Veracruz, where Americans controlled the docks and would have confiscated the cargo. For complicated legal reasons, the US could not seize the ship, and it docked at another port, Puerto Mexico (now reverted to its old name of Coatzacoalcos). The large cargo of weapons was unloaded and distributed to Huerta's forces (Naval History).

On April 25, the US occupation declared martial law and ordered that all weapons be turned in. Surprisingly, some 13,000 weapons and 150,000 rounds of ammunition were turned in. On April 27, transports arrived from Galveston with US Army troops, which would occupy the city until further notice. Most of the sailors and Marines returned to their ships. The American occupation of the port city would last seven months.

The US Army occupation forces were commanded by Brigadier General Frederick Funston, who, in the recent conflict in the Philippines, had led a patrol deep into the jungle to capture the elusive Emilio Aguinaldo, the leader of the Philippine Insurrection. Funston's heroism in that earlier colonial war was tainted by rumors of atrocity. However, he had redeemed himself by commanding the US Army detachments that helped restore order in San Francisco after the catastrophic 1906 earthquake. His successful administration of one port city after a calamity probably helped him successfully deal with another after a battle.

To many in the military, the choice of Veracruz seemed to indicate a much bigger campaign was in store. Many officers thought the occupation of Veracruz, as in the earlier Mexican War, was a prelude to an invasion of Mexico that would advance to Mexico City. They could see no other compelling reason for taking the city (Boot 153).

FORMAL RAISING OF FIRST FLAG OF US
VERACRUZ 2 PM APR 27.14

HADSELL
VERUZ
3149

The raising of the US flag over Veracruz.
https://commons.wikimedia.org/wiki/File:1914_Occupation_of_Veracruz.jpg

General Funston seems to have been very effective as commander in Veracruz. He cleaned up the city and worked to improve overall sanitation. Veracruz, like most cities on the Gulf of Mexico and the Caribbean, had for centuries been prone to outbreaks of yellow fever and malaria. Funston's cleanup sharply reduced the incidence of infectious diseases (Boot 153).

The fighting on April 21 and 22 cost the American force seventeen deaths and sixty-three wounded. Records are far from complete, but the Mexican side listed at least 126 killed and 195 wounded, and probably considerably more. The Americans killed during the battle for the city received elaborate funeral services. They were placed in caskets, each decorated with an American flag, placed on the deck of the battleship *Montana*, and taken to New York City. The battleship was met at sea by the presidential yacht, which saluted the dead. On arrival in New York, they were met by large crowds, placed on horse-drawn caissons, and taken on a slow funeral procession to the Brooklyn Navy Yard, where President Wilson gave a eulogy. The treatment was highly unusual and was not repeated (Naval History).

The fighting in Veracruz sparked anti-American mob violence in Tampico and other Mexican cities. US Navy and other nations' warships evacuated several thousand Americans and other foreign nationals, and a great deal of property owned by American businesses was damaged. Mayo had the humiliation of requesting that a German warship help rescue the Americans. There was also rioting in Mexico City targeting American businesses, but it was less severe than at Tampico—mostly broken windows. A statue of George Washington was pulled down (Boot 155).

American President Wilson demanded that Huerta step down. His policy was that the US would not leave Veracruz until Huerta ceded the Mexican presidency. Huerta refused, and the occupation of Veracruz had no noticeable impact on his administration. However, the large weapons cache from the *Ypiranga* didn't help. Huerta resigned on July 15, 1914, after his forces suffered a devastating defeat in June when Pancho Villa's army took the city of Zacatecas (Kohout).

Huerta was an intriguing and rather amoral character. His mother was Huichol, so his rise through the Mexican military was unusual. He was trained as an engineer and cartographer. Working his way up through the ranks, he eventually commanded forces that repressed a rebellion in Guerrero, a Yaqui rebellion in Sonora, and a Maya rebellion in Yucatan. Once, he had Pancho Villa arrested and ordered Villa to be executed, but the charges were ordered dropped by President Madero. Huerta's anger over this was likely related to his order to have Madero shot (Kohout).

Image of Pancho Villa.

General Huerta was crude and ruthless. In his seventeen months as a dictator, he had at least thirty-five opponents stood up against a wall and shot. President Woodrow Wilson's disapproval resulted in several American measures against Huerta, including the arms embargo. Huerta appears to have calculated that the American actions in Veracruz would arouse Mexican patriotism and strengthen his support. Mexican patriotism surged after the invasion, but support for Huerta did not.

Huerta did not quietly disappear. After stepping down, he and his family left Mexico from Puerto Mexico on a German cruiser, landing in Jamaica. From there, Huerta chartered a United Fruit steamer to Britain and moved to Spain. In Spain, Huerta envisioned making a comeback. He was contacted by German agents, who were interested in using Huerta to divert American attention from the developing crisis in Europe. Huerta sailed to New York City, where German agents and spies developed a plan for his reentry to the Mexican Revolution. (The US did not enter the First World War until 1917, so German agents remained active, although under surveillance.) The German operatives placed large sums of money in accounts Huerta could use to buy weapons and pay troops. Finally, Huerta boarded a train for New Mexico. His new rebellion was set for June 28, 1915 (Kohout).

When Huerta got off the train in New Mexico after the long trip, he was arrested by federal agents and jailed, charged with conspiracy to violate American neutrality. Over the next several months, he was in and out of jail and under house arrest in El Paso. His trial was set for mid-January 1916, but he died early in the month from cirrhosis of the liver.

Whether German intrigues successfully diverted American attention away from Europe can be only a guess. The famous Zimmerman Telegram of January 1917, intercepted by the British, proposed that Mexico join Germany in a military alliance against the United States and shows the Germans remained interested in Mexico. The telegram offered Mexico back the land it had lost in the Mexican War. The telegram was a major propaganda win for the Wilson administration, which wanted to intervene on the Allied side. It seems likely that Germany envisioned Mexico in the same terms as its alliance with the Ottoman Turks—an ally not particularly strong but capable of causing major headaches for the enemy.

The dark green was the territory of Mexico; the light green was what was promised to Mexico in the telegram.
NuclearVacuum, CC BY-SA 3.0 <https://creativecommons.org/licenses/by-sa/3.0>, via Wikimedia Commons; https://commons.wikimedia.org/wiki/File:Zimmermann_Telegram.svg

After the occupation of Veracruz ended, a peculiar controversy developed. It was claimed that the War Department had handed out Medals of Honor by the bucketful. It wasn't quite that bad, but the Veracruz intervention produced by far the largest number of these medals of any American battle in any war. Sixty-three Medals of Honor were awarded in the Veracruz intervention. Of these, fifty-three went to Navy personnel (who had just been made eligible for the award), nine to Marines, and one to a soldier in the Army. That compares to 126 medals awarded during World War I and 471 during World War II (Halton).

Smedley Butler, then a Marine major, was awarded one for heroism at Veracruz. Butler did not think he deserved the medal and tried to return it. The Navy said yes, he would keep it and yes, he would wear it if he wanted to continue being a Marine officer (Naval History).

Chapter 5: The Banana Wars in Panama

After Spain lost control of the mainland American colonies in the early 1800s, Panama became an isolated province of New Granada, soon to be named Colombia. Once, Panama had been the transit route for silver from Peru to Spain, and hence crucially important. Silver would be shipped from Peru to the Pacific coast of Panama, carried across the isthmus by pack mule, delivered to a port on the Caribbean, and loaded on annual treasure fleet ships for transit to Spain. The route was used for centuries. Although the ships were occasionally beset by English or French pirates, between 1550 and 1790, the immense wealth of the silver mines at Potosí in Upper Peru (now Bolivia) was shipped to Spain. American silver that crossed Panama financed the Spanish wars with the Ottoman Turks, the wars against the Protestants in Europe, and Spain's century of being a superpower.

Panama was never populated because malaria and yellow fever prevailed in the swampy lowlands. Disease killed off a high percentage of invaders and settlers alike. The arrival of the silver and the fleet were frantic annual events, bracketing a sleepy and pest-ridden backwater the rest of the year. Some of the population was descended from escaped slaves, and several indigenous peoples maintained a traditional life.

Panama remained isolated because reaching it by land from the rest of Colombia was almost impossible. The Darien Gap, a wilderness on the border of Panama and Colombia, was a trackless tangle of mountains, jungle, and swamp—almost impassible. To this day, it remains a roadless wilderness and a refuge for criminals and rebels.

As discussed, American interest in a canal across the Panamanian isthmus went back many years. In the 1830s, President Andrew Jackson sent an emissary to investigate a canal, but nothing came of it. By then, Americans were already involved in trade in California for tallow and hides. Panama became important once again due to the cession of California to the United States in the aftermath of the Mexican War. Of course, gold was discovered in 1848, and 200,000 people settled in California by 1850, overwhelming the Indian tribes and the small Hispanic population. While the immigrants came from places as far away as Mexico, Chile, Australia, and China, most came from the United States.

In 1847, even before gold was discovered at Sutter's Mill, a group of New York businessmen organized the Panama Railroad Company and got a concession from Colombia to build a railroad (Meditz & Hanratty).

Once news of the discovery of gold spread, tens of thousands of people all over the world got gold fever and the urge to go to California and make a fortune. To get to California in 1849, Americans had three choices. They could travel by steamboat to cities on the Mississippi or Missouri and go west by caravans of covered wagons powered by oxen or mules. They could leave from New York or New Orleans for the long sail around South America. Or, they could travel from an American port (usually New Orleans) to Panama's Caribbean coast, cross the isthmus, and take a ship to California from Panama City.

American entrepreneurs quickly organized the Panama route with steamers on both the Caribbean and Pacific, accommodations, and guides across Panama. This posed a problem because Panamanians spoke Spanish and were not always friendly. Diseases remained rampant, and occasional political chaos made the Panama route problematic, but tens of thousands of travelers used it anyway.

The Panama Railroad was not completed until 1855, with the first train making the complete passage in January 1856. Building the railroad required substantial capital and importing rails, engines, cars, and other necessities. One result was the rise of a new city at the Atlantic terminus of the railroad, which Panamanians called Colon, after the explorer Columbus. The Americans named it Aspinwall after one of the investors, but the Panamanian name prevailed. A footnote to this history is that the

Panamanians refused to deliver mail addressed to Aspinwall, accepting mail for the city only if the address read "Colon" (Medits & Hanratty).

The American government began subsidizing mail steamers using the Panama route in 1848. The mail subsidies were crucial, providing a steady income for the companies operating the ships. The two companies winning the mail contracts were the United States Mail Steamship Company, from New Orleans to Colon, and the Pacific Mail Steamship Company, from Panama City to California. The word "mail" in those names may have reassured travelers that they had some official connection to the United States. Travel through Panama was considerable early on and became a flood after the Gold Rush began. About 500,000 people transited the isthmus between 1848 and 1869. While people traveled in both directions, most traffic was to California (Daley).

It was not only people who crossed the isthmus. It took time for California to develop an infrastructure and more time to develop industry, although the state had adequate resources to feed and build housing for the huge immigrant population. Until California developed more fully, tools and machinery came by ship from the outside, and much of that came via the Panama railroad. People traveling to California usually brought large amounts of supplies and tools along on their trip.

One sad event with a wry name illustrates the kind of problems that could arise. On April 15, 1856, a bloody event occurred in Panama City, where 1,200 Americans were waiting for the *John L. Stephens* and other steamers to arrive and transport them to California. When the ships arrived, the travelers would be rowed out to board the steamships. Then, as now, people waiting for transportation got bored, and we can assume some alcohol was involved. In this incident, we know that a man named Jack Oliver was in the street in the evening hours and got a slice of watermelon from a street vendor. He didn't like how it tasted, so he spit it out. He refused to pay for it, and the vendor insisted he do so. The two got into a fight, the vendor with a knife and the American with a gun. Details are scanty, but an angry mob grew by the hour in what became known as the Watermelon Riot (Daley).

The mob attacked the hotels where Americans were staying and attacked American businesses. Many of the Americans had guns, part of the gear they had assembled for life in California, and fought back. The police were called out and joined the mob instead of trying to impose order. There was a pause, and then the mob attacked the railroad terminal. By the end of the riot, some of the hotels, the terminal, American businesses, and other structures were reduced to ashes from arson. At least fifteen Americans and two Panamanians were killed, and perhaps fifty more Americans were injured. Panama City was fearful that American filibusterers might attack and take revenge (Daley).

In response, the US sent a representative to investigate the situation. He called for the annexation of the isthmus. The Navy landed 160 men, who seem to have occupied a railroad station for a few days and then returned to their ship. The resident US consul saw the riot as the result of a drunk American being abused by a Black man. Panamanians saw it as provoked by arrogant Americans. Such differing points of view would become very common during the era of the Banana Wars in Panama and elsewhere.

The US did have treaty rights permitting intervention. In 1846, the US and the Republic of New Granada, as Colombia was then called, signed the Mallarino-Bidlack Treaty, which allowed American intervention in Panama in conditions of unrest.

The US government demanded reparations for the Americans killed and injured in the Watermelon Riot, and a commission was created to investigate the event and the claims. New Granada eventually accepted responsibility and paid $500,000 in damages (Daley).

Panama experienced a great deal of political instability, most of it a spillover from the chronic fighting between the Liberal and Conservative parties dominating Colombia. Some of the instability came from rivalries within Panama. From 1850 to 1900, Panama experienced fifty riots or rebellions, five attempted secessions from Colombia, and thirteen American interventions of various kinds. Colombia experienced coups and several wars, including the exceptionally bloody War of a Thousand Days from 1899 to 1900. Between 1863 and 1886, Panama had twenty-six presidents (provincial heads) with frequent coups and coup attempts (Meditz & Hanratty).

In 1885, some of the violence from Colombia spilled over into Panama, and there was serious rioting in Colon, the city created by the Panama Railroad. The situation was a bit complicated. Former Panama President Rafael Aizpuru proclaimed a revolt and captured Panama City, announcing he wanted to kill every American in Panama. On the other side of the country, a Haitian immigrant named Pedro Prestán, with an ideology of hatred for all whites, seized Colon.

The Colombian government requested American intervention, and the Navy landed 2,000 troops from eleven warships. They quickly captured Panama City, but Colon was nearly destroyed before the troops arrived. American troops occupied both cities and patrolled the railroad route. They captured both Aizpuru and Prestán, turning both over to the Colombians. The Colombians sentenced Aizpuru to ten years' exile and hanged Prestán (Boot 61).

After centuries of talk about a canal across the isthmus, in the 1880s, the first attempt occurred. The French adventure capitalist and entrepreneur Ferdinand de Lesseps got the concession for a canal from Colombia, with the provision that it had to be completed in twelve years. De Lesseps was the man behind the Suez Canal, which was completed in 1869 and dramatically changed the political situation in the Middle East. His reputation from Suez ensured that loans were readily available and stock in the company was easy to sell.

De Lesseps was not an engineer. He was a venture capitalist who was very good at convincing investors and organizing businesses. He formally began the project in 1880, but excavations did not begin until 1881. His company bought up most of the stock in the Panama Railroad, although keeping its American managers. Given Panama's labor shortage, thousands of laborers had to be brought in, mostly from the British West Indies. Some work on locks for the canal began in 1888.

De Lessep's company ran into two very serious problems. The first was that Panama's endemic diseases killed an estimated 25,000 laborers. The second was that corruption in the marketing of company stock and the need for loans brought the company to bankruptcy in 1889, when all work on the canal stopped. One reason may have been American interference. The US strongly opposed having a European power control a canal in Central America and seems to have interfered with loans. The French effort did accomplish a lot of work, completing about a third of the excavation needed for the canal, and some of the machinery left over was used by the Americans (Meditz & Hanratty).

Tensions with Spain brought home the need for an American-dominated Panama Canal. In 1898, the battleship USS *Oregon,* one of four of the most advanced American capital ships, was anchored at San Francisco, and the Navy wanted the ship to join the Atlantic fleet. At the time, Spain's fleet was thought to be powerful. The *Oregon* sailed around South America to join the Atlantic fleet in an epic voyage that covered

12,000 miles and took sixty-eight days. The distance would have been more like 4,000 with the canal. The *Oregon* participated in the naval battle at Santiago in Cuba, in which the Spanish fleet proved to be almost toothless and was totally outgunned and quickly destroyed. The American fleet had two casualties.

President Teddy Roosevelt had served as Assistant Secretary of the Navy not long before he assumed the presidency (he was vice president when President William McKinley was assassinated). He was strongly pro-Navy and was determined to have a canal, no matter what the Colombians, Panamanians, or Democrats in the US thought. The canal would mean warships could easily be shifted between oceans depending on threats posed. Even then, American strategists were most concerned with Germany and Japan. When the canal was built, it was designed to accommodate American warships. The canal was not built just for the convenience of the Navy, but it was a convincing argument for canal proponents. National security plus heightened commerce was an irresistible argument.

The construction of the Panama Canal resembles the earlier experience of the British and the Suez Canal, completed in 1869. The British had for many years used the overland route across Suez to the Red Sea and on to India, as the Americans used Panama to get to California. Suez immediately became a pivot point of British strategy. While the French had built it, the British wanted control and eased the French out by purchasing the khedive's (Egypt's ruler) shares. The US may or may not have hampered the French effort in Panama, but it was of intense interest to the American military.

British strategy to defend India required assured control of the Suez Canal. The canal gave the Egyptians a choke point if they chose to use it, which meant the British felt the need to eliminate the potential for the Egyptians to cause trouble. Egypt and what is now Sudan became British protectorates, Sudan because of its coast on the Red Sea. American strategy to protect California and the West Coast was somewhat similar (although California and the West were closely connected to the East by rail, so the parallel is inexact). But, getting battleships from one coast to the other was crucial while battleships were the decisive weapons at sea. So, like Egypt, Panama was fated to become a protectorate.

The origins of Panamanian independence are a bit foggy. The usual story is that the United States wanted a canal. Colombia dragged its heels, so the US sent in the Navy and got Panamanians to declare independence. The reality is a bit less imperialistic, but the US Navy's role was real.

Attempts at secession had happened several times in Panama's earlier past. Colombian representatives signed a treaty in January 1903, an agreement called the Hay-Herrán Treaty, but it was not ratified by the Colombian Senate. The treaty would have granted the US perpetual rights to a ten-kilometer-wide strip across Panama. For some reason, a revolutionary junta appeared in Panama, possibly because the Panama elite wanted the money from constructing the canal to remain in Panama, not diverted to distant Bogota. The junta gained control of Panama City and called for American assistance (Meditz & Hanratty).

Meanwhile, a Colombian ship carrying 300 or 400 troops landed at Colon. The manager of the Panama Railroad refused to transport the troops to Panama City, claiming mechanical problems. He did allow the Colombian commanders to travel to Panama City, where they were promptly arrested. On November 5, the USS *Dixie* appeared off Colon with secret orders to prevent reinforcements from landing in Panama, and none did. The *Dixie* landed Marines, and the Colombian troops declined the opportunity to fight. The Colombian officer in command decided to take the troops back to Colombia, a decision no doubt helped by an $8,000 bribe (Boot 134).

Whether the US recruited the rebels is unknown, but the Americans seemed to know about the secession attempt in advance. It is thought that the revolutionaries secretly contacted the Americans before acting (Meditz & Hanratty).

The newly-independent Panama promptly signed a treaty about the canal. It gave the US rights over a ten-mile-wide zone, extended three nautical miles from shore to allow for control of the near approaches. It also gave the US rights to control the land and water required for the canal to function. The treaty was ratified by the US Congress in January 1904. Panama was paid $10 million, and a $250,000 annual payment would kick in after the canal opened. The US paid the owners of what remained of the De Lesseps company $40 million for rights to the canal. Eventually, the US paid Colombia a $25 million indemnity (Meditz & Hanratty).

As in Cuba, the US insisted that Panama write into its new constitution the right of American intervention in any part of Panama to restore order. The Panamanians did not like the provision, but they had no choice. The US did intervene in disturbances in Panama in 1906, 1908, 1911–12, and

1915. The provision stood until 1933, when it was repealed by an agreement between Panama's president and the Roosevelt administration (Peace).

The American construction of the Panama Canal did not start from scratch. The abortive French effort had done about a third of the excavation, and the Panama Railroad had been running for decades. Building the canal was delegated to the US Army Corps of Engineers, headed by Colonel George Washington Goethals. The canal was an extraordinarily complex project, and devising the locks and how to fill them was especially difficult. Goethals proved to be something of a genius at running the overall effort.

Engineering was not the only major problem. There was another difficult aspect, a problem that had plagued Panama for centuries: disease. As mentioned, the estimated 25,000 laborers who died in the earlier French attempt to build the canal perished mostly from diseases. The diseases included malaria, yellow fever, typhoid, parasitic diseases, and other afflictions. Another member of the Corps of Engineers, Colonel William Gorgas, was assigned to improve sanitation and deal with these ancient killers (Meditz & Hanratty).

Gorgas did just that. He was just as much a genius at constructing public health as Goethals was at constructing the canal. He drained swamps, eliminated sites for mosquito breeding, constructed sewage systems for towns, and took other precautions based on the recent work of Walter Reed in the American occupation of Cuba. Disease was not eliminated, but cases were sharply reduced. The number of lives lost in the American effort to build the canal was about 5,000, apparently more from accidents than disease. Some historians think the total is much higher. Still, without Gorgas' work, the toll would have likely been equal to or higher than during the French attempt.

By 1913, 65,000 people were employed on the canal. About 5,000 were American engineers, administrators, and managers; some 12,000 came from Southern Europe, and the rest were from the Caribbean. How many men on the project were Panamanian citizens is unknown. The casual racial bias characteristic of the US at the time continued in the Canal Zone, where the racial hierarchy was strict. Within the Zone, African Americans and Afro-Caribbean laborers had segregated housing, water fountains, and latrines, just like the situation in the contemporary American South.

Inside the Zone, which was 550 square miles, conditions for American employees, civilian and military alike, were quite good. Conditions for the laborers were not so good, and in Panama City and Colon, slums developed. The Zone was, in effect, a foreign country, a slice of the United States dividing Panama in two.

Relations between the Canal Zone authorities and the Panamanian government varied. Panama was dominated by the canal but remained more independent than might be expected. There were disputes over payments and contention over merchandise purchased at Post Exchange (PX) stores in the Zone and smuggled out of the Zone to avoid paying taxes. Panama's government sometimes asked for American intervention, such as during rent riots in Panama City in 1925.

In 1913, United Fruit faced strikes in Costa Rica and labor unrest in Panama. The company's response was to bring in strikebreakers and then call for troops. In Panama, troops were at hand in the Canal Zone, where Marines formed part of the garrison.

Chapter 6: The Banana Wars in Honduras

Honduras in 1915 had only a half million people. Profitable American business in the country at first had nothing to do with bananas. The New York and Honduras Rosario Mining Company (NYHRMC) mined gold and silver. Americans had begun planting bananas in Honduras in 1889 when the Vaccaro Brothers company, headquartered in New Orleans, started a few banana plantations. At first, the crop was marketed only in the New Orleans region as an exotic tropical fruit. It took some time before the market grew (Merrill "Honduras").

The political situation in the country was chaotic. Between independence and 1900, there were 210 armed conflicts, civil wars, rebellions, and coups. In 1899, there was a peaceful and constitutional transfer of power from President Manuel Bonilla to General Terencio Sierra, the first uncontested transfer of power in decades. In 1903, Manuel Bonilla (no relation to the previous president, Policarpo Bonilla) staged a coup and became president.

Nicaragua was the most powerful of the Central American nations, despite its relatively small population. President Manuel Zelaya had been a dictator for years. Zelaya dabbled in Honduran affairs and supported Honduran rebels, some of whom crossed the border with help from the Nicaraguan army and established a provisional government. Early in 1907, Zelaya invaded Honduras, intending to overthrow President Bonilla—and did. This bothered the United States, which landed troops at Puerto

Cortes (near the Guatemalan border on the Caribbean coast) and elsewhere to deter Zelaya. The US called for a conference of all the Central American republics in Washington, DC, in April 1907, which was cosponsored by Mexico (Merrill "Honduras").

The five nations signed a General Treaty of Peace and Amity in late April. A compromise government was set up in Honduras, and the nations pledged to set up a Permanent Central Court of Justice to help settle disputes. They also pledged to restrict the activities of exiles from neighboring countries. It worked for a time.

Miguel Davila, the Liberal faction interim president of Honduras, was elected to the office and served from 1907 to 1911. The inevitable opponents tried to overthrow him in 1908, backed by El Salvador and Guatemala, with Davila strongly supported by Nicaragua. A war among the four countries seemed about to break out, but war was averted, and the Honduran rebellion collapsed (Merrill "Honduras").

In 1911, President Davila faced a rebellion by previous President Manuel Bonilla. The Honduran government fielded 5,000 soldiers, facing an unknown number of Bonilla's rebels. Bonilla's force was commanded by a colorful American soldier of fortune named Lee Christmas; the rebels also included another American, Machine Gun Malony, thoughtfully provided by Samuel Zemurray, president of Cuyamel Banana Company (Jewett 6).

American mercenaries had some importance in these myriad coups and rebellions. How many there were is unknown, as is their origin. Some may have been deserters from American forces and others just drifters. Lee Christmas was awarded the rank of general in the Honduran army when Bonilla won.

Honduras was struck by the same malady that characterized all the other countries of the region—debts too large to repay. Loans had been taken out from European and American banks, with the interest and principal to be repaid from customs receipts. Customs was the only steady and reliable income, but the collection of customs duties was inept and corrupt. Frequent coups and rebellions were expensive to deal with, and it was sometimes unclear what the legal government was.

In 1908, US President William Howard Taft brokered a deal. The US would set up a customs receivership under American management; a consortium of New York banks would renegotiate Honduras' debts and grant a large loan to pay them off. The American bankers were given control of Honduras' railroad system, and the US would guarantee Honduran independence. The deal resulted in a calm era until 1920 (Merrill "Honduras").

The calm was relative. There was still rivalry between the banana companies. They competed to open land for banana farms, and the Honduran government gave them sizable land subsidies. The banana companies came to control almost all the best land on the Caribbean coast. Towns like Trujillo became company towns, and the companies had as much or more local authority as the national government. The banana production regions and the company towns were near the Caribbean coast, which made it relatively easy for American naval intervention if it came to that.

Not all problems resulted in military intervention. In 1917, a dispute arose when the Cuyamel Banana Company extended its railway to the Guatemalan border. Guatemala, where United Fruit was strong, moved troops to the border. United was apparently concerned that Cuyamel might start buying bananas in Guatemala. American representatives negotiated a settlement agreeable to all sides.

In 1917, a major strike against Cuyamel was crushed by the Honduran army at Cuyamel's request. In 1918, another strike broke out against United Fruit at La Ceiba, Honduras, where United had a concession. The Honduran government arrested the strike leaders, and the US sent a warship just in case violence broke out—a cruiser with enough crew and Marines aboard to send a sizable force ashore. The strike collapsed when Cuyamel offered wages equivalent to $1.75 a day (Merrill "Honduras").

Perhaps the strikes were an indication that the calm era was over. Between 1920 and 1923, Honduras experienced seventeen uprisings and attempted coups. Some tension was rising among the countries, so in August 1922, the presidents of Honduras, Guatemala, and El Salvador met aboard the American cruiser USS *Tacoma*. The result was another conference of Central American presidents in Washington, which resulted in another Treaty of Peace and Amity. The representatives pledged to restrict the activity of exiles from neighboring nations in their countries. It also limited the Honduran army to 2,500 men.

It didn't work so well. In 1924, Honduras experienced a rebellion caused by a dispute over who should be president. United Fruit supported one of the claimants, a man named Tiburcio Carías. In February 1924, a battle broke out at La Ceiba in which fifty people were killed, including an

American citizen. US Marines landed at several places in Honduras to protect American citizens and property, but there was little other violence. The US sent Sumner Welles, a prominent American diplomat, to solve the problem. Welles managed to get the different sides to meet aboard another US Navy cruiser, where a deal was thrashed out (Merrill "Honduras").

Honduras experienced another period of relative calm. The Depression hit Honduras hard, and the market for bananas crashed. In 1931, President Mejía Colindres had to borrow $150,000 from the banana companies to pay his army.

Chapter 7: The Banana Wars in Guatemala

Guatemala and Honduras both wanted to attract investment and offered land and tax privileges to attract banana companies. Minor Keith first got involved in Guatemala to finish a railroad but got interested in growing bananas there and demanded concessions, which he got. The political conditions in the country were favorable for United Fruit. As the result of a coup in 1899, General Manuel Estrada Cabrera became dictator and ruled until 1920 with a harsh but steady hand.

Guatemala has had a deep social division since colonial times. Early in the 20th century, two-thirds of the population were Maya. The country also had a small Afro-Guatemalan population on the north coast. The Maya people had stubbornly resisted Hispanicization for centuries, and most had maintained their language and much of their traditional culture. Many spoke Spanish and were Catholic. The country was run by elite families, with little Maya participation. Other than the elite, the politically active portion of the population, were the *ladinos*, of mixed origin but defined simply as people who spoke Spanish and had adopted the Hispanic culture and lifestyle. Most ladinos were poor, but they were considered Hispanic and therefore superior to the Maya. Under the Barrios dictatorship (1873–1885), government policy was to try to force the Maya out of subsistence farming by manipulating taxes and labor laws. One method was to levy taxes that had to be paid in cash, which could only be obtained by working.

While politics within the Central American republics was chaotic, sometimes their relationships were equally troubled. One nation might support a rebellion against a neighbor or even invade. In 1906, El Salvador invaded Guatemala. It's one of those wars poorly known outside the region, and it ended in a stalemate. Yet at the main battle at El Jícaro, the Salvadorians lost 700 and had 1,100 wounded, and the Guatemalans are thought to have lost 2,800 (Jewett 5).

As with several other Central American nations, the population was concentrated in the highlands and the Pacific side of the country. The government wanted to build communication with the Caribbean coast but had few resources, so they welcomed United Fruit. That part of the coast was loosely attached to Guatemala and close to the Mosquito Coast, which was a British territory with undefined borders that could claim areas in Guatemala and Honduras.

When United Fruit began to develop banana plantations in Guatemala, a major problem was a lack of labor. To remedy this, Black laborers were imported from Jamaica and the United States, particularly from the region centered on New Orleans. This was a large labor migration, involving about 20,000, and created several problems. Laborers from Jamaica and the British colonies were not used to the kind of Jim Crow discrimination that was routine among American United Fruit managers. The sharp increase of Black people led to resentment among local Hispanics, who disliked the flood of Black English speakers and had a local tradition of discrimination. Some of the American laborers returned home, and some migrated to the interior of Guatemala, where there was bias but discrimination was considerably milder (Colby 603).

The use of Black labor from the United States also posed a problem for the US State Department. Black Americans were second-class citizens, but they were still citizens, so if a Black laborer was harmed by some kind of incident in Guatemala, how should the government react? The issue was posed when several Black American men were beaten by a Guatemalan mob (Colby 603-04).

The Jamaicans were more assertive than African Americans, having come from a British colony where discrimination was less rigid. They also seem to have had a negative attitude toward Hispanic culture. The ladinos returned the attitude, and in 1910 there was a disturbance involving 600 Jamaicans. Ladinos got involved and lynched one Jamaican. The dictator declined to break strikes, preferring negotiations, but did not hesitate to use force when he thought it necessary (Abbott 16).

United Fruit did do a considerable amount of good in Guatemala. They built sewage systems for towns, drained swamps for mosquito control, built reasonably good housing for workers and excellent housing for their managers, poisoned areas where mosquitoes bred, and even built hospitals and schools. They rebuilt Puerto Barrios, imposing a grid system and turning the place into a company town. The main motivation was the health and convenience of their managers and administrators, not so much for laborers.

The company also imposed American-style segregation. No laborers were permitted to enter the front yard of any white person, and they were to doff their hats when talking with a white person. Little was done for the health and convenience of the laborers, whether they were Black or Hispanic. Workers suffered high rates of tuberculosis and pneumonia.

In 1909, some disturbances occurred when the company reduced pay. United Fruit called for President Estrada Cabrera to quash the disturbances, and he did so, sending in 200 troops. Soon Guatemalan soldiers were posted on or near almost every plantation, paid for and housed by United Fruit. What was low wages for the imported American and West Indies laborers was attractive to ladinos, thousands of whom migrated to the banana zone. The company used a wage differential and separated housing by groups to keep tension between them, which prevented them from joining together and striking (Colby 611-12).

The government broke several strikes, and United Fruit continued to produce bananas in Guatemala. The basic issues continued even though the Good Neighbor Policy had mostly ended military interventions. In 1954, what might be called a modernized banana war occurred with the government of the mildly socialist Jacobo Arbenz. United Fruit owned hundreds of thousands of acres in the country in 1954 but utilized only a fraction of them, while thousands of rural peasants remained landless. United had all that land as insurance in case Panama disease struck and existing plantations had to be destroyed and new ones planted. The Arbenz government seized what they considered to be surplus land to distribute to the peasants. United Fruit appealed to Washington, which acted. Washington was worried about the spread of Communism, and the seizure of United Fruit's land was considered evidence of Communism.

No Marines were sent, but the newly-formed Central Intelligence Agency (CIA) acted, sponsoring a coup that ousted Arbenz and installed a military dictatorship. The military government was exceptionally harsh, and the impact of a generation of repression following the coup still affects the country.

Chapter 8: The Banana Wars in Nicaragua

American interests in Nicaragua went back long before the welter of Banana War interventions. In 1849, Railroad magnate Cornelius Vanderbilt (for whom Vanderbilt University would be named years later) got rights to a railroad route between the Atlantic and Pacific coasts of the country. For twelve years, he was also given the right to build a canal connecting the coasts. Vanderbilt's enterprise was named the Accessory Transit Company. The canal would have used Lake Nicaragua and other waterways and remains the most logical route for a new canal (Merrill "Nicaragua").

In 1850, the British tried to block Vanderbilt's company, and violence was orchestrated by each side. As a result, the British and Americans agreed that any future canal would be open to the shipping of both countries. The British maintained control of the port of San Juan del Norte (which was not yet incorporated into Nicaragua). Americans would have control of the route, hotels, and other related resources.

Another American influence in Nicaragua was highly negative. In 1855, American filibusterer William Walker invaded and took over the country. (A "filibusterer" was a cross between a pirate and a soldier of fortune, from a Dutch word for pirate. They were mercenaries, not just soldiers; some were interested in power.) Turning Nicaragua into an English-speaking American colony seems preposterous today, but in 1855, the country was weak, poor, and thinly populated. A large influx of American colonists and their slaves might have been able to do this, the way Texas became Anglo-American in the 1820s and 1830s.

Walker had been invited into the country by defeated Liberals. With a few hundred mercenaries and followers, he seized the capital after defeating the country's army. He declared the national language to be English and legalized slavery. He may have hoped it would be annexed to the United States. His government was recognized in 1856 in the US by the Franklin Pierce administration. (Merrill "Nicaragua").

Walker set up a puppet president and began planning colonization by Americans. He also made a serious mistake: he took over Vanderbilt's company assets. So, Vanderbilt helped get rid of him. Vanderbilt gave Costa Rica funds to offer Walker's men free passage back to the United States. Costa Rica seized the steamers on Lake Nicaragua, reducing Walker's mobility and communications with the outside. In 1857, Walker declared himself president.

Walker appears to have been a good soldier and won several battles while taking control of the country and resisting attacks from the outside. Guatemala, Honduras, and El Salvador allied to oust Walker, which Costa Rica later joined. The alliance invaded Nicaragua, and Walker beat off the attack, but it was obvious his game was up. The captain of an American warship brokered a deal that allowed Walker and some of his followers to leave. He returned to the US in May 1857 (Merrill "Nicaragua").

Walker tried to make a comeback in each of the next four years. In 1860, he ran out of luck. He was intercepted by a British warship, captured, and turned over to Honduras. The Hondurans promptly put him in front of a firing squad. The episode roiled the already tempestuous politics of the Central American nations. The war to oust Walker was moderately bloody, with about a thousand killed on each side.

When the century turned, Nicaragua had another dominating personality: José Santos Zelaya, the dictator of Nicaragua from 1893 to 1909. He was ruthless with opponents, but as dictators go, he was something of a liberal, building much-needed infrastructure, including schools. He took control of the Mosquito Coast in 1894, which ended centuries of informal British rule. (The Mosquito Coast was an odd combination of the descendants of escaped slaves and indigenous tribal peoples, sustained by cutting hardwoods.)

Where Zelaya caused problems for his nation and others was his strong opposition to the Panama Canal. He thought that the best route would have been through Nicaragua. In his opposition, he courted Germany and Japan to see if they were interested in the Nicaragua route for a canal. It's unclear how far this interest went, but Zelaya could hardly have done anything more to make the United States suspicious of him (Merrill "Nicaragua").

In February of 1907, the armies of El Salvador and Honduras joined with Nicaraguan Liberals who had rebelled against Zelaya and invaded Nicaragua. In a short battle, Nicaraguan machine guns mowed down between 2,000 and 3,000 of the invaders (Jowett 5).

In 1909, Zelaya faced a rebellion in Bluefields, a place controlled by the British for decades. It was the Nicaraguan headquarters for many foreign companies doing business in the country, including companies in gold mining, rubber harvesting, and bananas. The dictator had given concessions to his supporters and cronies, which conflicted with the claims of foreign business. His army advanced on Bluefields, capturing two American nationals and executing them. Zelaya's policies had already resulted in intense American disapproval. Zelaya realized that if he did not leave, the Americans would intervene, so he resigned and had one of his supporters, José Madriz, installed as president. The Zelayista forces were advancing on Bluefields, and the rebel in Bluefields, General Juan Estrada, told the international community he could not hold the town (Boot).

This is the point where a Marine officer named Smedley Butler entered the Banana Wars and, because of his involvement, became an enduring legend. Although he became a larger-than-life figure, he was only five-foot-nine and weighed 140 pounds. He came from a Quaker family of considerable influence. His father and grandfather served in Congress, and his father served for years on the House Naval Affairs Committee. Father and son worked to save the Marines, and Smedley Butler's exploits helped save the Corps from a miserly Congress intent on abolishing the Marines.

Butler wasn't interested in attending a university. He lied about his age and enlisted in the Marines at 16. He was too late to fight in Cuba but did in China during the Boxer Rebellion and in the Philippines during the Philippine Insurrection. In China, a bullet that should have hit his heart was deflected by a brass button, which he carried as a souvenir of his luck.

He caught typhoid in Asia and Chagres fever in Central America and survived both. He took a year off to recover and ran a coal mine in West Virginia, sharply increasing its profits. Butler rejoined the Corps as a major and was stationed in Panama, commanding the 3rd battalion of the 1st Marines. From there, he was called to intervene in Bluefields, where 300 rebels faced 1,500 Zelayista troops. Butler and some Marines landed at the town and ran the Zelayistas off with sheer bravado (Boot 100-104).

The Zelayistas faded, but the problems in Nicaragua continued. After a few presidents failed, in 1912, Adolfo Díaz was elected. He needed money, so he agreed to an American receivership of Nicaraguan customs. The State Department arranged a loan of $1.5 million through a group of New York banks. In return, they obtained control of the national bank and the country's railroad and steamship line. In July 1912, General Luis Mena, the war minister and a member of the Liberal Party, launched a revolution. Mena's faction was successful and besieged the capital, Managua. On August 4, American President Taft ordered 100 sailors to Managua to protect the US legation. On August 11, the rebels bombarded the capital, killing hundreds. On August 14, Major Butler and his 334-man Marine battalion arrived in Managua, and the rebels backed off (Boot 146-47).

By September, there were 1,100 Marines in Managua. Butler's exploits included taking a train into rebel-held territory, mounting machine guns on top of the cars. Arriving at a town occupied by the rebels, Butler's men were attacked by cavalry—men on horseback attacking a train armed with machine guns, like something out of a B-grade movie. Butler and a few Marines battled the large rebel force, which disintegrated. Butler reached Mena, the rebel general, and convinced him to seek refuge in Panama. The Marines then pulled out of the country, leaving 100 to guard the American legation.

The Banana Wars were more intense in Nicaragua than elsewhere in Central America. The main reason was Augusto Sandino, the barely five-foot tall son of a plantation owner and an Indian servant who was a charismatic and wily leader—and hated the US Marines. Sandino was the most formidable rebel leader Americans faced during the Banana Wars.

Major corporations became interested in Nicaragua in the late 1800s when American and British companies entered the country and set up companies to exploit Nicaraguan resources—timber, rubber, gold, and then bananas. The US bankers Brown Brothers and J & W Seligman &

Co. advanced another loan to the Nicaraguan government in return for control of Nicaragua's railroad and national bank.

In 1916, the US and Nicaragua signed the Bryan-Chamorro Treaty, giving the US exclusive rights to build a second canal and the rights to naval bases. (A century later, this could still be the route for a new canal to replace the aging Panama Canal.) The 1916 treaty was likely premised on denying other nations the possibility of constructing a canal rather than Americans building a second one.

After the downfall of Zelaya in 1909, Nicaragua embarked on a period of instability. The United States generally supported Conservative party governments. In the early 1920s, a civil war erupted over a disputed presidential election, but the violence was quickly contained.

There was another Marine incursion into Nicaragua in March 1927 when Brigadier General Logan Feland led 2,000 Marines into the country to protect American interests. Yet another war had broken out between the Conservative Party government and the Liberal Party opposition. The US also sent in a top diplomat, Henry Stimson, a former Secretary of War. During an extended visit in April and May of 1927, Stimson negotiated an agreement in which both sides agreed to elections in November 1928 (Bettez).

The deal that Stimson brokered was called the Pact of Espino Negro. By its terms, the rebels and army would disarm, and the US would train a nonpartisan military force. Adolfo Perez would finish the terms of the exiled president, Carlos Sólorzano, and elections would be held in 1928, supervised by the US. The Americans set up and trained this new national paramilitary force, the *Guardia Nacional* (National Guard), which quickly developed into a quality constabulary and was, for a time, nonpartisan.

Not all Nicaraguan factions agreed. Sandino, who had fought in the civil war on the Liberal side, made it plain that he would fight against the agreement, founding an armed group and calling it the Army for the Defense of Nicaraguan Sovereignty (Merrill "Nicaragua").

Augusto Sandino was an eloquent and charismatic leader. His past was complicated; he killed a man in some kind of quarrel and had to flee the country. He went to Honduras, where he worked in an American-owned sugar company, then moved to Guatemala, where he worked on a United Fruit banana plantation. He went on to Tampico, then a boom town from oil wells. He seems to have been radicalized during his stay in Tampico, where socialism was running strong among Mexican oil workers (Boot

235).

Sandino moved his small but growing force to El Jícaro, a small village in the remote province of Nueva Segovia, and modestly renamed it Ciudad Sandino (Sandino City). The American forces in the country, about 1,100 Marines, made plans to suppress Sandino.

Sandino made a major mistake that cost him heavily. In July 1927, he attacked the town of Ocotal, which was garrisoned by forty-one Marines and forty Nicaraguan National Guards and reinforced by a column of seventy-five Marines and seventy-four guardsmen. Ocotal was a town of about 1,800 people in a poor defensive position. Sandino decided this was the time to attack, and he anticipated victory. The Sandinista force tried to infiltrate Ocotal on the night of July 15, but an alert Marine sentry detected the effort and sounded the alarm. The infiltration failed, but Sandino still ordered attacks the next day (Boot 236)

The rebels outnumbered the garrison at least six to one, and assaults on the town were unrelenting. The garrison was heavily outnumbered but far better armed. One unusual aspect of this battle at Ocotal, which proved decisive, was the use of Marine aircraft: five DH-4 biplanes, a British design. Each plane had two machine guns and could carry several small bombs.

Two of the planes attacked the Sandinistas on the morning of the initial attack, and later in the day, all five of the planes appeared over the battlefield. The aircraft repeatedly strafed and dive-bombed Sandino's men. This was one of the first times in military history that aircraft were used in close air support of ground troops, which would become typical of Marine operations in later wars. The air attacks were something Sandino's men had never before experienced, and they broke the Sandinistas' attack. Sandino pulled back and retreated. The Marines and guardsmen only had one casualty and one wounded despite the intensity of the fighting. The Sandinistas suffered at least sixty deaths, probably more (Boot 237-38).

On October 18, 1927, Sandino's men shot down a Marine aircraft, capturing the pilot and gunner, who they put on trial and then shot. Sandino anticipated a Marine operation to try to rescue the fliers. A Marine-led patrol was quickly sent out, and Sandino ambushed it, forcing it to retreat, killing four guardsmen in the process.

Marine operations continued to be frustrated. In mid-December, two columns of Marines and guardsmen started a march intended to reach and destroy Sandino's headquarters, which had been moved to a remote mountaintop. Both columns ran into intense fire and had to retreat. One of the columns, 174 Nicaraguan guardsmen and Marines, retreated to the small town of Quilalí. They were surrounded there by Sandino's force. They held on under heavy fire and had unusually heavy casualties—eight killed and thirty-one wounded. Marine aviation was again a feature. A Marine aviator, 1st Lieutenant Christian Schilt, made ten flights over two days onto a makeshift landing field under heavy enemy fire. He delivered supplies and evacuated eighteen wounded. The airplane had no brakes, so Marines had to run to the plane and grab the wings to slow it down on landing. The lieutenant won a Medal of Honor for these actions. Sandino broke off the action (Boot 240). The next month, a larger force worked its way to Sandino's remote headquarters and found it abandoned.

Sandino's rebels set up a regional base using classic guerrilla tactics, terrifying local residents and companies. The Sandinistas collected taxes and threatened savage punishments on anyone who dared to cooperate with the government forces or the Americans. Cooperation was enforced by machete, and the Sandinistas did not hesitate to execute opponents (Brooks 320-21).

There was a split among Americans regarding what strategy to use against Sandino to protect the 1928 elections. Which was best: hunting him down or stationing Marines in cities and towns to prevent guerrilla interference with the voting? The strategy of occupying towns was used, and 5,000 American troops monitored the election on November 4, 1928. Nicaraguans elected a new Liberal Party president, General José María Moncada, who succeeded Adolfo Díaz. At the time, Americans congratulated themselves that it was the first honest election in the history of Nicaragua. Given the country's tumultuous political history, it might even be true. There hasn't been one as honest since.

Nicaragua at that time was inhabited by less than a million people. Like other Central American countries, most of the population lived on the Pacific side, west of the mountain chain in the central part of the country. The eastern, Caribbean side was lightly populated, and some inhabitants were native peoples who had no sense of being Nicaraguan. This included the Mosquito (or Miskito), part of the same groups inhabiting British Honduras and the Mosquito Coast. The Marines found the natives useful allies in making deep patrols into the jungle (Brooks 315).

The Nicaraguan part of the Mosquito Coast was not formally part of the country until 1894, when the dictator Zelaya marched into the area. The British were not interested in war, so they negotiated and settled the issue. Some of the traditional Mosquito habitat was the Rio Coco, the longest river in Central America forming much of the boundary between Honduras and Nicaragua. The river flowed through dense jungle and had its source in the mountains in the central part of the country, excellent for guerrilla fighters. The natives knew it well, and adding them to mobile and well-armed patrols traveling light helped the Marines eventually reduce Sandino's effectiveness, although they never ran him to ground.

The election was a success, but Sandino's resistance continued. Aggressive small unit patrols didn't track him down. On New Year's Eve, 1930, Sandino ambushed a Marine patrol, killing eight of the ten men. He then shifted his focus to the Caribbean coast, raiding American-owned businesses, including a United Fruit banana plantation. United Fruit and other American businesses urgently requested help and received an entirely new kind of response. Secretary of State Stimson told them they had to rely on the Nicaraguan government. If that wasn't enough, then they should leave (Boot 247).

The conflict continued at a lower level but sometimes flared up. On December 28, 1932, a ceremony was planned to celebrate the completion of a railroad connection. The outgoing President, Moncada, was to drive a golden spike. The Marines and guardsmen were tipped off that Sandino was planning to raid the ceremony. A group of seventy guardsmen under the command of a Marine, Lewis Burwell "Chesty" Puller, boarded a train and headed for the site. (Puller was an aggressive and charismatic officer, like Smedley Butler; later, he was a prominent general in the Pacific Theater in World War II and Korea.) The train pulled into the site where the ceremony had been scheduled and found hundreds of Sandinistas looting the place. A firefight erupted and decimated Sandino's men, killing thirty-one of them. However, the defeat did not end Sandino's resistance (Boot 249-50).

US Marines with Sandino's captured flag.

When the last American troops finally left Nicaragua in 1933, Sandino agreed to disband most of his force and work with the government. Sandino and the government agreed that he would be allowed to retain 100 armed men and a base in the remote north. Some 1,800 Sandinistas were demobilized.

The Marines never got to Sandino, but other Nicaraguans did. On February 21, 1934, Sandino was invited to a formal dinner at the presidential palace. Sandino's party left about 10:00 p.m., but soon after, their car was stopped by a roadblock, which had been arranged by the head of the Guardia, Anastasio Somoza. Sandino and his two companions, former officers in the Sandinista forces, were captured and taken to a nearby airfield. Sandino's brother was also there, abducted earlier. The four men were machine-gunned to death. Somoza staged a coup a few years later, and the Somoza family ruled the country for the next forty-two years.

Chapter 9: Banana Wars in the Islands: Cuba

In 1898, Cuba, along with Puerto Rico, the Philippines, and some small island chains in the Pacific, were all that remained of Spain's once immense empire. Cuba was the most valuable—and troublesome—portion of what remained. Cubans rebelled several times in the 1800s. The rebellion from 1868 to 1878, called the Ten Years' War, ended in a crushing defeat for the rebels and took an estimated 200,000 lives. A smaller rebellion in 1879-80 was quickly put down. The rebellions did result in some reforms: slavery was abolished in Cuba in 1886, and Cuba obtained some representation in the Spanish *Cortes* (legislature).

Yet another Cuban rebellion broke out in 1895. This was the rebellion in which the Cuban patriot and poet José Martí was involved. He spent time in exile in New York City and Tampa, making many American friends, and his poetry was popular. He was killed in combat with Spanish troops in Cuba in 1895. Spain sent the formidable and ruthless General Valeriano Weyler to Cuba in 1896. Weyler is most known for his *reconcentrado* policy of emptying the countryside of Cubans, placing them in camps, and then shooting anyone in the countryside as a rebel. (The policy was applied in the most disaffected provinces.) This policy gave the world the words "concentration camp." Weyler was known as *El Carnicero*, "The Butcher." Tens of thousands of Cuban lives were lost in the camps and the fighting. Weyler was recalled to Spain in 1897, and the concentration policy was discontinued.

Spanish repression of the Cubans aroused American sympathy. Newspapers used the war to fuel subscription wars, whipping up war fever with the idea that the US had a moral obligation to help the rebels escape from a perfidious Spanish yoke. The battleship USS *Maine* was sent to Cuba as a show of force. On February 15, 1898, the *Maine* blew up in Havana harbor from unknown causes, killing 260 of the crew. What caused the explosion is still debated by historians. At the time, most Americans thought it was done by the Spanish.

The US used the *Maine* incident to justify declaring war on the Spanish on April 21. American troops left Tampa and landed in Cuba, fighting several battles with Spanish troops. On July 3, the Spanish fleet in Santiago harbor—four armored cruisers and three destroyers—tried to make a run for it, but all were beached or sunk in the resulting battle. The war ended on August 13, 1898, leaving the US in possession of Puerto Rico, Cuba, the Philippines, and Guam. American casualties were light, with about 2,000 deaths, mostly from tropical diseases.

One piece of American legislation was vital to the war in Cuba. An American senator named Henry Teller of Colorado added an amendment to the declaration of war against Spain. Known as the Teller Amendment, it stated that the US had no intention of annexing the island and would leave when pacification was achieved.

In 1901, Senator Orville Platt of Connecticut added an amendment to an appropriations bill that gave the US the right to intervene in Cuba to preserve order. Known as the Platt Amendment, it replaced the Teller Amendment and, in effect, gave the US the right to intervene whenever it wished. The amendment also required that Cuba get American approval for any treaty with another nation, keep foreign indebtedness low, and allow long-term leases for American naval bases. Apparently, Senator Teller agreed with Senator Platt's amendment. The Platt Amendment remained in effect until it was repealed in 1934.

What to do with these new possessions was the subject of intense political debate in Washington. By a narrow vote, the US decided to keep the Philippines until it was thought to be ready for independence and let Cuba become independent, with some conditions. Puerto Rico and Guam remain American territories to this day.

Post-war Cuba was devastated by the recent rebellion, which began before the damage of the Ten Years' War had been repaired. Infrastructure had been heavily compromised, hundreds of sugar plantations were harmed or destroyed, and many public buildings such as schools had been damaged. Food production was way down, and much of the island's wealth had been destroyed. The American occupation's first task was making sure Cubans didn't starve.

During the war, Cuban rebels had harassed the Spanish forces. When the war was over, Americans retired the *insurrectos* with a payment of $75 each. American forces occupied Cuba until 1902, ruling in cooperation with Cubans, but the US military was clearly the boss.

As the new Cuban legislature worked on a constitution, the Americans insisted that the Platt Amendment be written into the document. Cubans protested, but under threat that the US forces would not leave otherwise, it was duly added to the constitution. American troops left Cuba in 1902. The Platt Amendment was used to justify four separate American occupations of Cuba, which were not simply exercises in overturning unfriendly governments. Cuban governments called in American help to stave off rebellion, and anything that threatened American sugar plantations also threatened many of the Cuban elite, who profited from the sugar economy (Peace).

The military occupation did have some very positive results. Fortunately, the second military governor, General Leonard Wood, was competent. Wood, governor of part of Cuba and later military governor of the island, was a physician and did a great deal to improve health. He cleaned up garbage collection, a first for Cuba, and worked on installing sewer systems and access to potable water. Public health quickly improved, particularly when Walter Reed began measures to control mosquitoes, considerably lowering incidents of yellow fever and malaria. General Wood, however, tended to be authoritarian. Cubans who broke the sanitation regulations might be publicly whipped (Langley 7).

An image of Leonard Wood.
No restrictions;
https://commons.wikimedia.org/wiki/File:Leonard_Wood,_administrator,_soldier,_and_citizen_(1 920)_(14579077497).jpg

The occupation also built and rebuilt hundreds of schools. Cuban education under the Spanish regime had been relatively good. Americans translated books used in American schools into Spanish for Cuban students. The Ohio method was the model, emphasizing a basic education in reading, writing, math, and vocational training (Langley 10).

Cubans were less fond of the US Navy's insistence on choosing a location for a base on the island, although the Platt Amendment allowed for this. The Navy looked closely at Santiago, Havana, Nipe Bay, and Guantánamo. It seems to have preferred Havana, which horrified many Cubans; they appealed to President Roosevelt, who told the Navy Havana was off limits.

The Navy choose Guantánamo as a base because of its proximity to the strategic Windward Passage between eastern Cuba and Haiti. The passage was important for centuries (and still is) because it is a main route for shipping from the Atlantic into the Caribbean. It became even more strategic with the construction of the Panama Canal (Langley 28).

The American occupation and friendly Cuban presidents saw American investment in Cuba skyrocket. Americans bought up sugar mills and gained contracts for city services and a railroad. Minor Keith of United Fruit bought 200,000 acres near Nipe Bay for $400,000. The escalating American investment in Cuba also escalated the likelihood of American intervention to protect American-owned businesses when political violence threatened Cuba.

Elections were held in December of 1901, resulting in the election of Tomás Estrada Palma as president. American troops left following Estrada Palma taking office. Cuban politics were chaotic and highly volatile. In a plainly fraudulent election, Estrada was re-elected president in 1905.

A revolt against Estrada began in August 1906, leading to the second American occupation of Cuba. Earlier in his presidency, Estrada had signed legislation that allowed the US to lease Guantanamo Bay, and he lowered the tariffs on American products entering Cuba. Many Cubans disliked his pro-American stance. American investors and Americans involved in Cuba's vitally important sugar industry strongly supported the president. So, when he requested American support to deal with the rebellion, they supported him.

In a complicated political maneuver, Estrada resigned from the presidency in September 1906. Cuba was left without a president, and that provided the rationale for the second American occupation of Cuba. On

October 6, 1906, American troops landed in Cuba. More than 5,000 troops were involved, calling themselves "The Army of Cuban Pacification."

US President Roosevelt had sent a commission headed by Secretary of War William Howard Taft to investigate and see if negotiation could settle the problems; it did not. Following Estrada Palma's resignation, under the terms of a 1903 treaty, Taft became interim governor. On October 12, a civilian, Charles Magoon, was appointed governor of Cuba. Magoon had previously served as governor of the Canal Zone. He was unpopular with most Cubans, and there were unsubstantiated accusations of venality. One positive accomplishment was that Magoon offered an amnesty that largely ended the rebellion (Peace).

In January 1909, Magoon turned over the government of Cuba to the newly-elected president, José Miguel Gómez. The second American occupation of Cuba ended, and American troops were withdrawn.

At the time of the American withdrawal, Cuba's economy was in turmoil with high unemployment, and protests occurred, especially in Oriente province in eastern Cuba. Poverty was so extreme that many poor farmers had to sell their land, which was eagerly bought up by American speculators interested in setting up more of the quite profitable sugar plantations. Some smallholders lost their land because of insecure titles and even simple theft.

One group badly affected by unemployment and chronic bias was Afro-Cubans, who were a relatively high portion of Oriente's population. Slavery had lasted until 1886 in Cuba, and discrimination remained strong. In 1906, an activist named Evaristo Estenoz founded the *Partido de Independiente de Color*, the Independent Colored Party or PIC. The Cuban government outlawed the party in 1910 but did not crush it. In May 1912, Estenoz launched a rebellion in Oriente, joined by about 10,000 followers.

The rebels attacked some American sugar plantations and burned a town. Cuban President Gomez requested American intervention. The Cuban establishment seems to have had concerns that the rebellion would turn into a race war of the kind that had devastated Haiti a century before. On June 2, 2,600 Marines landed in Cuba and spread out, garrisoning towns and sugar plantations and starting the third American occupation of Cuba.

The Marines protected infrastructure and urban areas, allowing the Cuban army to go after the rebels. The repression was brutal, characterized by massacres and summary executions. There are no reliable records, but somewhere between 3,000 and 6,000 people were killed in Oriente, most of them Afro-Cuban. When he was captured, Estenoz was summarily executed, and his movement was wiped out. With order restored, American troops left Cuba on August 2. This is counted as the third American occupation of Cuba, but it was short and mild, and the Cuban government continued in authority.

Political conditions in Cuba remained volatile. In November 1916, President Mario García Menocal claimed victory, but the election was rigged. The Liberal Party rebelled in early 1917, led by former President José Miguel Gomez. The rebel forces quickly grew to 30,000, and Menocal's presidency was in grave danger. However, Menocal was strongly pro-American, and the US supplied his forces with weapons. Finally, Marines were sent in, landing on February 12, 1917, not long before the US declared war against Germany.

The rebellion faded away, and there was little combat between the rebels and the Americans. The occupation forces protected sugar plantations, mines, and other facilities. Part of the American motivation was to ensure the supply of sugar, which considered important for the war economy.

Cuban politics continued as usual for the first years of the occupation, with the Marines assuring that no rebellions would occur. This occupation did not at first feature an American military governor or Americans running the Cuban economy. Menocal won re-election in 1920, but the corruption and fraud were so evident that in 1921, the occupation authorities stepped in and took over Cuba's government.

On June 6, 1921, General Enoch Crowder arrived on board the battleship USS *Minnesota*. He was officially described as a "special representative of the president" but was really a military governor. Crowder's experience went back to the 1880s in Arizona when he was involved in the fights against the Apache chief Geronimo. For two years, Cuba was governed from the decks of the *Minnesota*. Crowder set up elections and also tried to reform the Cuban economy (Peace).

Cuban elections took place, and General Crowder stepped down, becoming ambassador to Cuba. The Marines, except for the usual legation guards, left in 1923. American efforts to impose order on Cuban elections had minimal impact. General Machado y Morales was elected president and established himself as a near-dictator. Cuba remained closely connected to the American economy, with two-thirds of Cuba's sugar crop processed in American-owned mills and Americans owning more than a fifth of Cuban land (Peace).

Cuba also became affected by American crime connected to the era of Prohibition (1920–33) when the production, sale, possession, and use of alcohol were prohibited in the United States. Cuba is close to the US, and during Prohibition, Havana became a wild party spot for Americans craving alcohol and entertainment. American gangsters smuggled alcohol from Cuba into the US and gradually came to operate in Cuba (although the mob heyday in Havana was later, in the 1950s).

Cuba fell under the domination of a dictator who was at first a power behind the throne but emerged as the strongman, Fulgencio Batista. He ruled Cuba from 1934–44 and 1952–59, when a revolution headed by Fidel Castro overthrew him.

Chapter 10: Banana Wars in the Islands: Haiti

Hispaniola is the large Caribbean island with Cuba in the west and Puerto Rico to the east, shared between Haiti and the Dominican Republic. The island's history is unusual in that Haiti was a French colony during colonial times, while the Dominican Republic was Spanish. Little trace of the centuries of Spanish rule remains in Haiti. Spain ceded Haiti to France in 1697, and it was known in French as Saint-Domingue. The French quickly developed Haiti's plantations for sugar and coffee. For many decades, Haiti was the largest producer of sugar and the most valuable colonial possession in the world, producing a huge amount of sugar through an efficient and ruthless form of plantation slavery, as well as a large amount of France's total income. In 1790, Haiti had 30,000–35,000 whites, 25,000 mixed-race people, and 500,000 slaves.

The French Revolution of 1789 infected Haiti, eventually resulting in a massive slave rebellion. The British intervened, and Napoleon sent an army of 75,000 soldiers to suppress the rebellion. Disease and war killed many people in a war characterized by extreme atrocity. The French army experienced an estimated 70,000 deaths, and the British lost the lives of 40,000 soldiers and sailors. Something like 25,000 white colonists and an unknown number of mixed-race creoles died, along with perhaps 200,000 slaves. All told, the butchers' bill was 350,000 lives. It was the only successful slave rebellion in history, but the cost was tremendous.

France eventually recognized Haitian independence but imposed an indemnity of 150 million francs that crippled the Haitian economy for many decades and took more than a century to repay, bleeding the Haitian economy of the equivalent of billions of current dollars. Haiti experienced chronic political instability, although it had several remarkable dictators, one of whom conquered the Dominican Republic, which Haiti ruled from 1822 to 1844.

Haiti had a rough 19th century. The war for independence killed off half the population and destroyed most of the infrastructure, including almost all the sugar industry that had made the colony so important to France. There was prolonged violence between contenders for power and the war of independence that ended Haitian occupation of the Dominican Republic. France threatened to reconquer Haiti, averted only by the island nation agreeing to an enormous indemnity that France demanded as reparation for damage inflicted during the struggle for independence.

The United States did not formally recognize Haiti until 1862. Haiti possessed a site that would have made an excellent navy base, Mole Saint-Nicolas, which some American naval officers badly wanted. In 1870, President Grant proposed annexing the neighboring Dominican Republic, but the US Senate rejected the proposal (Haggerty "Haiti"). However, there were several American interventions in Haiti in the 1800s. American intrusions, usually US Navy warships appearing at Port-au-Prince to protect Americans or American property, occurred in 1857, 1859, 1868, 1869, 1876, 1888, 1892, and several more times between 1900 and 1911 (Peace).

Political instability was common in the country. Between 1843 and 1915, only one of twenty-two rulers served a complete term, and several were assassinated. There were 102 civil wars, coups, or revolts during that span. Haiti was run by the elite, who were largely urban, mostly mixed race, and descended from French and African roots. The rural peasantry was mostly Black, and relations between the two groups were sometimes strained. The elite tended to see the rural peasants as uneducated bumpkins (Boot 157).

Haiti is about 10,000 square miles, some of it rugged mountain country good for growing coffee—and for guerrillas. In 1915, the country had a population of around two million. The capital and center of politics and the economy is Port-au-Prince, which had a population of around 60,000. The population was predominantly rural and engaged in subsistence agriculture, with some fishing, seasonal migration to work as laborers in sugar plantations elsewhere, and a few banana and sugar operations. Although Haiti had been independent since 1804, the culture was (and remains) strongly influenced by France. Members of the country's elite families were often schooled in France and spoke both French and the dominant Haitian Creole (commonly called Kreyòl).

Americans had been suspicious of German activity in the Caribbean since the 1903 crisis in Venezuela, and German activity in Haiti aroused concern. American suspicions about German expansion went back more than a decade. German and American warships came very close to a shooting battle in Samoa in 1889, but a typhoon intervened and sank three German and three American warships. The Germans had been interested in the Philippines and, after the Spanish-American War, bought the remaining parts of Spanish Asia—the Caroline, Marshall, and Mariana Islands.

As for German activity in Haiti, in 1897, German gunboats enforced a demand for indemnity because a German had been expelled from the country in a legal dispute. In 1903, another episode of German gunboat diplomacy occurred when a German warship intervened in a Haitian rebellion. The German ship found a Haitian gunboat that had interfered with a German merchant ship, but the Haitian vessel blew itself up to avoid capture (Haggerty "Haiti").

The German warships did not appear in Haiti's waters by coincidence. There were about 200 German residents in Haiti, several of whom had married into influential Haitian families. This allowed the Germans to become Haitian citizens and evade the constitutional provision that no foreigners could own Haitian lands. In one way or another, Germans controlled about 80 percent of Haiti's overseas trade. Germans owned utilities in Port-au-Prince and Cap Haïtien. German nationals owned a small railroad, warehouses, and other facilities. The US State Department took an extremely dim view of this (Military "Haiti").

As with other nations in the region, Haiti had debts it could not pay back—not just the loans but even the interest due. The debt was to European and American banks, although it is unclear how the indemnity to France for damages fit into the debt. In 1910–11, the State Department arranged for a consortium of New York banks to loan Haiti enough to pay the debt. The condition was that the banks take control of the Banque Nationale de la République d'Haïti.

Haiti's legally elected president died in an accident in 1912. Five men struggled for power, ending only when General Vilbrun Guillaume Sam took power in March 1915. President Sam almost immediately faced another rebellion and took hostages. American intervention, which led to an extended occupation of the country, began in 1915. The precipitating incident was the death of the pro-American Haitian President Sam in July. The president was facing opposition and had 167 political prisoners shot. Most were from elite families, and the public reaction was extreme. A mob invaded the presidential palace and literally tore him to shreds, triumphantly exhibiting Sam's mangled body in public after the killing (Military "Haiti").

American views of Haiti were made worse by the casual racism of the era. The US Secretary wrote about the people of Haiti: "The experience of Liberia and Haiti show that the African race is devoid of any capability for organization and lack genius for government. Unquestionably there is in them a tendency to resort to savagery and cast aside the shackles of civilization" (Peace).

With that kind of casual bias at the center of the US government, it's no surprise that occupation began, but it is surprising it ended. Still, the fact that it was the longest American occupation during the Banana Wars is no surprise.

On July 28, 1915, American warships landed 330 Marines in Port-au-Prince. The Secretary of the Navy ordered the troops to protect American and European interests and nationals from possible mob attacks. Another reason appears to have been to avoid the election of an anti-American president to replace Sam. After President Sam had been assassinated, rebels were in the process of taking over the government. The rebels were about to control the capital when the Marines arrived, and they pulled back when the Americans threatened to bombard the city.

The American military government declared martial law in 1915, and it lasted until 1929—an unusually long period for martial law to apply. It may be the longest period of martial law in American history. Haiti had no legislature from 1917 to 1930.

US Marines defending a gate in Haiti in 1915.
https://en.wikipedia.org/wiki/File:American_Marines_In_1915_defending_the_entrance_gate_in_C ap-Haitian_-_34510.jpg

Haitians generally refused to fill many government positions in an American-run occupation of their country. As a consequence, Marine and Navy personnel often filled civilian administrative jobs. Haitians who did accommodate the American occupation suffered scorn from more nationalist Haitians and faced racism from Americans running the country.

The US military governor of Haiti was Admiral William Caperton. He chose Philippe Sudré Dartiguenave as Haitian president, but all Haitians working for the government had minimal power. Caperton declared martial law on September 3, allowing the arrest and detainment of "troublemakers."

Dartiguenave was not always particularly happy about being the American's puppet. In one incident, he was required to sign a treaty giving the Americans rights over most of Haiti's governmental functions, but he balked at it. A marine officer, Smedley Butler, took a squad to the presidential palace. The president was disinclined to meet with Butler and locked himself in a bathroom. The story (which may or may not be true) is that Butler found a ladder, leaned it against an outside wall, climbed to the bathroom window, opened it, and found the President sitting, in formal top hat and tails, reading a popular magazine. Butler is said to have climbed in through the window and presented Dartiguenave with the treaty and a fountain pen (Boot 161-62).

The puppet Haitian legislature adopted a new constitution that passed in a referendum by a 98,225 to 768 margin, which suggests the occupation monitored the voting. The new constitution was written by an American politician named Franklin Roosevelt. A key provision was that foreigners could now buy land in Haiti, reversing a policy that had stood since 1804. The change was strongly resented by Haitians (Military "Haiti").

After the US declared war on Germany in 1917, German assets in Haiti were confiscated, eliminating competition with Americans. German nationals were interned. There was some American investment in sugar plantations, but the overall investment was light and not particularly profitable.

A unique feature of Haiti was a group called the Cacos, best defined as a hereditary class of peasant rebels endemic to the mountains. They were part-time brigands, as well. They dated back to rebel slave warriors during the independence wars of 1789–1804. Their relationship to the chaos of Haitian presidential politics is unclear, and is not well understood. Regardless, the Cacos provided much of the opposition to the American occupation and fought two wars with them.

Smedley Butler and other aggressive Marine officers took the war to the Cacos, who were concentrated in the mountainous and remote north. They routed a large Caco force at the small port town of Gonaïves. The Caco redoubt was on a mountaintop at Fort Rivière, apparently once a French post. Captain Butler and twenty-six Marines made their way through the scrub and stormed the fort. The Cacos heavily outnumbered Butler's small force but had almost no modern weapons. The only American casualty was from a rock thrown by one of the Cacos. About fifty of them were killed in the assault. The rebels learned they could not win in a face-to-face battle with the far better-armed Marines (Boot 61-62).

Butler was tasked with training a new paramilitary force called the Gendarmerie d'Haiti. The object was to create a trained and nonpartisan force loyal to the American occupation. One important element was that most of the recruits were Black Haitians, who willingly suppressed rebel groups that were mixed race. Butler was given command of the force.

The lack of Haitian cooperation led the American governor to disband the legislature. To do that, he had to obtain the signatures of the president and cabinet. The technical term is "prorogue," and legally only the president could prorogue the Haitian legislature. On January 19, 1917, Butler and some of his gendarmes went to the presidential palace and browbeat Dartiguenave into signing a document disbanding the legislature, which did not meet again until 1929.

In Haiti, resentment of the American occupation was widespread, and the Marines had to use what were described as "chastisement" methods. The methods involved combat patrols, early morning police raids, confiscating property, and killing cattle. The occupation revived the practice of corvée labor—forced, unpaid labor on roads and other public projects—using a Haitian law dating to 1864. In theory, the forced laborers were provided adequate food, housing, and transportation and worked for a specified period, but these conditions were not always met.

The Marines brought with them contemporary American attitudes about race. Haitian history had been characterized by mixed-race people dominating politics and culture and not always sympathetic to the plight of the urban or rural poor. The American occupiers made no such distinction—a Haitian was a Haitian—an attitude that helped forge a sense of common Haitian identity based on opposing the occupiers (Hagerty "Haiti").

In 1918, a massive rebellion occurred, estimated at 40,000 participants. The Marines put it down with the assistance of the newly recruited and trained Haitian Gendarmerie. Casualties among the Americans were low, but as many as 2,000 Haitians may have died during the rebellion's repression (Haggerty "Haiti").

A mixed-race Haitian named Charlemagne Péralte had been arrested on a minor charge in Port-au-Prince but escaped into the countryside. He was a French-trained lawyer but managed to appeal to the Cacos and gather a sizable number of them—as many as 5,000—to begin a resistance movement against the Americans.

In October 1919, Péralte was tracked down and killed by a Marine patrol in a complicated ruse reminiscent of the capture of Emilio Aguinaldo in the war with the Philippine rebels. Péralte was eliminated, but the Marines made one very serious mistake with him. His body was tied to a door and carried back to the base to prove he was killed. A Marine officer decided it would make a good propaganda image to show Péralte dead, as an example of what happened to rebels. The resulting photograph showed Péralte's body in a Christ-like crucifixion pose. In Catholic Haiti, this had deep resonance and the opposite effect of the Marine's intent. The image is still used in anti-American propaganda more than a century later (Peace).

Péralte was replaced by his second in command, Benoît Batraville. The Americans launched an operation to eliminate the Caco resistance, using

1,300 Marines and 2,700 Haitian gendarmes. The campaign used aircraft with primitive bombs; explosives were placed in mailbags and dropped.

Batraville captured a wounded Marine, took him to camp, and beheaded him, cooking the man's heart and liver for his men to eat. Batraville did this to absorb the prisoner's courage and wisdom in a kind of voodoo ceremony. A Marine patrol got a tip from a peasant and attacked Batraville's camp. Batraville was wounded and shot—possibly while trying to surrender. With the two leaders killed, the second Caco war ended (Boot 175).

Marine enforcement could be harsh. Captain Smedley Butler (later a Marine major general) years later described the campaign against the rebels as brutal. The Marines were well-armed, and the rebels were not. Butler described how, after a failed Caco ambush, angry Marines hunted them down "like pigs" and killed at least seventy-five (Peace). In January 1919, Major Clarke Wells supposedly executed nineteen rebels. The details are foggy, but Haitians believed it, and stories of the incident sparked the rebellion led by Charlemagne Péralte.

The American public was turning isolationist, and sentiment was growing against the occupation as stories of cruelty and atrocity circulated. The stories were grossly exaggerated but had a basis in fact. In one small community in northern Haiti, an American officer killed two Haitians just for the fun of it. He was arrested and confined to a mental institution. Rural Haitians did not protest much because the American occupation brought an era of relative peace, with the Cacos subdued or eliminated (Boot 179).

Another bloody incident had a larger impact. In 1929, at Les Cayes, Marines fired on a peasant march, killing at least ten people. This resulted in a great deal of criticism, and President Herbert Hoover set up a commission to investigate the situation. He appointed W. Cameron Forbes to head the commission, and it traveled to Haiti. The Forbes Commission concluded that the US military occupation had done some good things but had shut Haitians out of any real authority, causing anger and opposition (Haggerty "Haiti"). The mixed conclusions made by the Forbes Commission were the beginning of the end of the occupation. The next US president was the man who had written the Haitian constitution of 1915: Franklin Delano Roosevelt.

Most of the Marines left Haiti in 1932, with a few not departing until 1934. By the time they left, the official body count was 146 Marines and

3,000 Haitians. However, the Haitian total can be assumed to be considerably higher. In 1934, Roosevelt initiated the Good Neighbor Policy that emphasized friendly relations among the American (in the broader sense) nations.

In 1935, new President Sténio Joseph Vincent seized power in Haiti. He corrupted the Gendarmerie by replacing its officers with his supporters. The Gendarmerie became a tool for the president to control the opposition—and Haiti.

Chapter 11: Banana Wars in the Islands: Dominican Republic

The American intervention in the Dominican Republic had much to do with American President Woodrow Wilson. The president was notably racist in his views of African Americans, and he viewed the mixed-race populations of the Caribbean and Central America as uncivilized and primitive. Wilson saw the role of the United States as one of teaching these other nations how to become better—in his view, "better" meant more like the US He amplified the Roosevelt Corollary beyond simply disciplining debtors, wanting to teach them to "elect good men." And in his view, there weren't many good men ruling in the Caribbean (Veggeburg 1).

The Republic of Wilson's time was mostly populated by the rural peasantry, and the total population was about 800,000. The first national census was in 1920 and showed 895,000 people. The capital city, Santo Domingo, had perhaps 20,000 people. The city is the oldest continuous European city in the Americas, dating to 1498. During Spanish times, the colony was generally called Santo Domingo. The city of Santo Domingo had once been important in the network of ports and fortresses that helped protect the annual Spanish fleets from the New World to Spain, but by the later 1700s, that role had faded along with the fleets, and the colony had long been a backwater.

The Dominican Republic is just under 19,000 square miles, not quite twice the size of Haiti. The country has an unusual history in having two independence dates: the first marking independence from Spain in 1821 and the second independence from Haiti in 1844. Haitian rule was probably more oppressive than Spain's, and there was no love lost between the two countries during the Banana Wars era. (The name "Dominican Republic" goes back almost to independence, but in the Banana Wars era, it was often referred to as "Santo Domingo" in English.)

The Dominican Republic's political history was one of a great deal of turmoil. For the twenty years after the Republic threw out the Haitian occupation force, two men alternated as president, with frequent fighting between their partisans—General Pablo Santana and Buenaventura Báez. In 1861, the economy was devastated. At the same time the Spanish government under Leopoldo O'Donnell was advocating renewed colonialism, some conservatives appealed to Spain to ask for annexation. The result was that Spain occupied the Republic from 1861 to 1865. The Americans were too busy with the Civil War to intervene under the Monroe Doctrine. Spanish rule did not improve conditions as the conservatives had hoped. A war for independence began, and Spain renounced the annexation and left the island in 1865 (Haggerty "Dominican").

This means that the country underwent three foreign occupations in a century: Haiti (1824-44), Spain (1861-65), and the United States (1916-1924). By 1914, the country had experienced forty-three different presidents and nineteen constitutions in the previous seventy years.

The Republic had a competent, if ruthless, dictator in Ulises Heureaux, who ruled the country from 1888 to 1899. He imposed peace, brought in Cuban sugar planters displaced by the Ten Years' War, and quietly took out loans from European and American bankers. Heureaux's style of rule can be judged from one incident. He invited an opponent to a magnificent formal dinner in the presidential palace and afterward brought out some fine cigars. After both lit up, Heureaux said, "Enjoy it; it will be your last. I'm ordering you shot after you are done." The dictator was out for an evening walk in 1899 when he was assassinated (Langley 20).

A revolution in 1899 produced a rare outcome: an honest election. Juan Jimenez Pereyra was elected president. However, a crisis developed when the Dominican Republic could not pay back loans when European bankers began calling them in. There was only one significant source of income, from customs. Jimenez promised that 40 percent of the customs duties would be used to pay interest and principal on the loans. That angered an American company, the San Domingo Improvement Company, which had also made sizable loans to the country and had been given authority to administer customs to assure repayment. This company complained to the US State Department (Haggerty "Dominican").

Political instability continued. There were coups in 1902 and 1903 and an uprising in 1904. Collecting customs taxes was difficult under such conditions. In 1905, the US negotiated an accord to take responsibility for the Dominican debt, collect all the revenue, and then allocate the funds to pay the debts and the government. Ramon Caceres, president from 1906 to 11, negotiated the deal with the US, and for several years, the county had competent rule. On November 19, 1911, as he was out for his usual evening ride in Santo Domingo, he was murdered (Haggerty "Dominican").

The assassination of Caceres resulted in a civil war, and he was followed as president by Eladio Victoria y Victoria, who served as president from December 1911 to November 1912. American collection of customs dues stopped, but American property was threatened. So, American President Taft sent in a commission to investigate, accompanied by 750 Marines. President Victoria stepped down and was replaced by an interim president, Archbishop Adolfo Alejandro Nouel y Bobadilla. The archbishop did his best to be neutral and stepped down in 1913.

Over the next several years, Dominican politics were chaotic, with almost revolving presidents. José Bordas Valdes served from April 1913 to April 1914. He was followed by Ramón Baez, who served from July to December 1914. Then came Juan Isidro Jiménez (who had been president once before), who served from December 1914 to May 1916, followed by Francisco Henríquez in 1916, who was pushed aside by the American invasion (Haggerty "Dominican").

US President Wilson demanded that Jimenez give Americans control of the Republic's finances, dissolve the nation's army, and form a constabulary commanded by an American. Jimenez was in an impossible position, facing American demands on one side and, on the other, opponents more than happy to describe him as an unpatriotic friend of the Americans (Veggeberg 3-4).

The Dominican Secretary of War, Desiderio Arias, tried to take power. But the US had stationed several warships at Santo Domingo, and Admiral William Caperton threatened to bombard the city. Arias evacuated it. Marines landed in the Dominican Republic in May 1916 after rivals deposed President Jimenez. They quickly defeated armed rebels at Las Trincheras and Guayacanas and occupied the city of Santiago.

Most Dominicans refused to join the American administration because it would have been political suicide—and possibly fatal. All the current Cabinet members resigned, so the US Navy was tasked with governing the nation. Marines were distributed across the Republic in small garrisons to control the countryside and keep order.

In 1916, the Navy Department assigned Admiral Harvey Knapp as military governor, and the US Navy ruled the Dominican Republic under martial law. The occupation did do some useful things. The Navy built bridges, improved the miserable system of roads, and suppressed violence. However, few Dominicans were put in positions of authority, and the occupation censored the press, radio, and public speeches (Haggerty "Dominican").

There were no powerful leaders of the Dominican resistance like there were in Haiti or Nicaragua. One local strongman, Vicente Evangelista, achieved some success, but he made the mistake of executing two American civilians. He was captured in July 1917, and a few days later, he was shot while trying to escape. At least, that's the official story (Boot 170).

The literacy rate in the Dominican Republic was low, and the economy was tied to subsistence, with some sugar exports. In some areas of the countryside, local strongmen dominated society, and these men led resistance to the American occupation. Armed resistance occurred almost entirely in the two eastern provinces of El Seibo and San Pedro de Macorís (usually just called Seibo and Macorís). The resistance level increased when, in 1918, American entry into World War I required a substantial drawdown of Marines from the island. A rebellion from 1918 to 1921 proved difficult to suppress.

In Seibo and Macorís, the Marines initiated a policy of separating the guerrillas from the rural population by setting up camps near or in towns and forcing the rural population into them. The countryside would then become what was called a "free fire zone" in the later Vietnam War. The technique had been used in Cuba in the 1890s by Spanish General Valeriano Weyler in the *Reconcentracion* policy. The fighting in Seibo and Macorís was far smaller in scale and far less bloody, but the principle was the same.

Just how severely the Marines repressed Dominican resistance may never be completely known. In August and September of 1918, Marine Captain Charles Merkel tortured and killed Dominicans found outside the concentration camps in Seibo. Somehow his crimes were reported to his superiors, and he was arrested. Someone had smuggled a pistol into his cell, and Merkel shot himself in his prison cell to protect the honor of the Corps (Folse).

After the Americans left, a key development fraught with importance for the country was the creation of a national police force, the *Guardia Nacional Dominicana*. This developed into a well-trained and well-armed force, at first with American officers. The Guardia helped American occupation forces repress the rebellions and was responsible for law and order in the countryside.

In 1919, the United States entered an isolationist phase, best remembered by the American Senate refusing to allow the US to join the League of Nations that President Wilson had pushed so hard to create. The mood also began shifting against American occupation of Haiti and the Dominican Republic. Several American newspapers accused the Marines of indiscriminate killings and the occupation generally of white supremacist views. Some of the accusations were accurate. The white supremacist views had a military impact in Haiti, leading the Marines to grossly underestimate the Haitian ability to organize effective resistance (Folse).

A new governor was sent to the Dominican Republic in 1921, Admiral Samuel Robison. His administration was considerably more effective. To crush the Dominican resistance in 1921 and 1922, under Marine General Harry Lee, the Marines shifted tactics from small patrolling units to cordoning off areas and sweeping them with larger units. Portable radios had become available, still bulky but greatly facilitating communication with troops in the field. This may have been the first use of radios for communication in combat. The Marines also began to use close air support, a characteristic of Marine operations ever since. These tactics were coupled with the offer of amnesty, which brought in 200 guerrillas. Lee also announced a policy of releasing imprisoned guerrillas for good behavior. By the end of March 1922, General Lee declared the Dominican Republic pacified (Veggeberg 14-15).

US Marines in the Dominican Republic in 1922.

As the occupation proceeded, American public opinion became less supportive of involvement abroad. With the improvements in administration, the increased willingness of Dominicans to join the government, and the end of armed resistance, conditions for ending the occupation appeared good. A Dominican politician named Francisco Peynado went on his own accord to Washington and met with Secretary of State Charles Evans Hughes. They worked out an agreement, the Hayes-Peynado Accord, which specified terms for the Marines leaving. The terms included five Dominican leaders choosing a provisional president, setting up national elections, and procedures for turning over police powers to the Guardia (Veggeberg 20).

The Dominican committee appointed Juan Batista Vicini Burgos as interim president, and the Marines left on September 18, 1924. There were no incidents, and there was no opposition to the departure. The Guardia took over policing duties under the new interim president's orders.

As in American occupations in Cuba and elsewhere, a special effort was made to improve sanitation in the two main cities, Santo Domingo and Santiago, where yellow fever and malaria had made city living during the fever season highly dangerous. As mentioned earlier, this wasn't altruism because eliminating mosquito habitats and thus cutting down on fever prevalence prevented debilitating illness and fatalities among American forces and administrative civilians. Whatever the negative impact on the Dominican people, the occupation somewhat improved overall health and the national infrastructure (Folse).

Conclusion: After the Banana Wars

In 1933, Marine Major General Smedley Butler had just retired. His thirty-three years in the Corps included involvement in American interventions in the Philippines, China, Nicaragua, Panama, Honduras, Mexico, and elsewhere, and serving in France in World War I. With two Medals of Honor and other awards, he was the most decorated Marine in the history of the Corps at the time.

His most sensational act was his testimony before Congress in 1934. In it, he claimed that prominent American business leaders approached him in a plot to stage a coup d'état to remove President Franklin Roosevelt from office and install a military dictatorship. Whether there was any truth to Butler's claims has never been established, and it remains a contentious topic. Had it occurred, it would have been like bringing the Banana Wars back home and would have profoundly changed American history.

Of more lasting impact, and quoted widely since, was a 1933 speech and later book in which Butler described himself as being an enforcer for big business:

"I spent most of my time being a high class muscle-man for Big Business, for Wall Street and for the Bankers. In short, I was a racketeer, a gangster for capitalism." About the Banana Wars, he said: "I helped make Mexico, especially Tampico, safe for American oil interests in 1914. I helped make Haiti and Cuba a decent place for the National City Bank boys to collect revenues in. I helped pacify Nicaragua for the international banking house of Brown Brothers in 1909-12" (Butler).

Notable in Butler's speech is using words like "racketeer" and "muscle man." The phrasing he used is from the vocabulary used in the 1930s to describe organized crime. Remarkably, Butler described himself and the Corps as behaving like criminals in the service of business. This was the era of Bonnie and Clyde, the St. Valentine's Day Massacre, and Machine Gun Kelley, and was not long after Al Capone went to Alcatraz prison for his depredations while running the Chicago mob (The charges against Capone were actually tax evasion and violation of the Prohibition laws).

The legacy of the Banana Wars has generally been negative. Still, the various American occupations usually had positive results in terms of building roads and bridges, constructing schools and hospitals, and improving public health. One positive result of the banana trade in Central America was that Banana Sam Zemurray, of the Cuyamel Fruit Company and then president of United Fruit, made a huge fortune and gave much of it away. Among his philanthropies were the medical school at Loyola University of New Orleans, establishing an inter-American agriculture college in Honduras, The New School for Social Research in New York, and the Boston Symphony.

The paramilitary forces the Americans trained and equipped were designed to be politically neutral, along the lines of a national constabulary. However, they also provided ideal platforms for future dictators.

After the Americans pulled out of the Dominican Republic, the *Guardia* was the strongest institution in the country. In 1930, its director, Rafael Trujillo, organized a coup d'état that placed him in control, and he typically ruled through puppet presidents. His dictatorship was notable for its ruthlessness and brutality. In 1937, he ordered the army to kill all the Haitians in the Dominican Republic they could find in what has come to be known as the Parsley Massacre. (Haitians seasonally migrated to work as laborers in the Republic.) Estimates of the number of Haitians massacred range from 20,000 to 30,000.

In Nicaragua, Somoza consolidated his control of the National Guard and then took over the country. He held an election for his chosen puppet president, who won by an announced vote of 107,201 to 108 (Merrill "Nicaragua").

Decades after leaving Haiti, Americans had to intervene again, almost ironically to clean up the havoc caused by some of their protégés from the Banana Wars era. François (Papa Doc) Duvalier took control of Haiti in

1959, and his son, known as Baby Doc, continued the family rule until 1977. American troops were back in Haiti in 1994 and may return.

In the Dominican Republic, Rafael Trujillo was assassinated in 1961, apparently in a CIA plot, because his heavy-handed tyranny had become an embarrassment. He had put down several rebellions but was careful not to damage American-owned property. The strong American bias against Communism enabled Trujillo to describe his opposition as Communist, generating American support rather than intervention. American troops were back in the country in 1965.

The Somoza dictatorship in Nicaragua was far worse and more authoritarian than any Americans had interfered with during the Banana Wars. Ironically, the Somoza dynasty was toppled in 1977 by a group calling itself the Sandinistas. The last Somoza dictator went into exile in Paraguay; he was assassinated there in 1980 by a Sandinista squad.

World War II seriously disrupted the banana trade. German submarines prowled parts of the Caribbean in the first year of the war, and although oil tankers were their preferred prey, they sank any ship they could. Losses in the Atlantic to German submarines early in the war were so significant that a serious shipping shortage arose; many of the ships previously used in the Caribbean were transferred to the vital Atlantic route that kept Britain supplied with food and Lend-Lease weapons from the US. Bananas were considered a luxury, and for the war years, mostly disappeared from American grocery shelves. The European market ceased to exist.

United Fruit continued in the banana industry and, by 1954, controlled perhaps 85 percent of the land in the American tropics suitable for growing bananas. Unfriendly governments and Panama disease forced the company to regroup, and it eventually renamed itself Chiquita Brands International (Jansen).

Another little-known result of the American interventions in the Banana Wars was their effect on American military doctrine in dealing with insurgency and how to conduct counterinsurgency operations. The Marines' experience in the Banana Wars era was central to the writing of the *Small Wars Operations* manual in 1935, which was revised in 1940 and retitled *The Small Wars Manual*, which governed counterinsurgency operations until 2008 (Halton).

While historians consider the 1934 Good Neighbor Policy the end of the Banana Wars, it was hardly the end of American interventions.

American concern about Communism increased, from the massive Palmer Raids in 1919 to the Army-McCarthy Hearings in the early 1950s. Americans sometimes intervened secretly to topple governments perceived as radical or socialist.

Here's another book by Captivating History that you might like

Free Bonus from Captivating History (Available for a Limited time)

Hi History Lovers!

Now you have a chance to join our exclusive history list so you can get your first history ebook for free as well as discounts and a potential to get more history books for free! Simply visit the link below to join.

Captivatinghistory.com/ebook

Also, make sure to follow us on Facebook, Twitter and Youtube by searching for Captivating History.

References

Abbot, Roderick. "A Socio-economic History of the International Banana Trade, 1870-1930. European University Institute, Florence, Italy, 2009. EUI working paper RSCAS 2009/22. https://cadmus.eui.eu/bitstream/handle/1814/11486/rscas_2009_22.pdf?sequence=1

Abbott, Roderick. "A Socio-Economic History of the International Banana Trade, 1870-1930." EUI Working Paper RSCAS 2009/22/ European University Institute, Florence, IT, 2009.

Bettez, David. "Cooperation and Conflict During a Banana War." Naval History Magazine 31 (4) August 2017. Retrieved May 30, 2023. https://www.usni.org/magazines/naval-history-magazine/2017/august/cooperation-conflict-during-banana-war

Boot, Max. The Savage Wars of Peace: Small Wars and the Rise of American Power. New York: Basic Books, 2002.

Brooks, David. "US Marines, Mosquitoes and the Hunt for Sandino: The Rio Coco Patrol in 1928." Journal of Latin American Studies 21 (2) May 1989. 311-42. JSTOR access May 28, 2023.

Bucheli, Marcelo. "Enforcing Business Contracts in South America: The United Fruit Company and Colombian Banana Plantations in the Twentieth Century." The Business History Review 78 (2) Summer 2004. 181-212. JSTOR access June 2, 2023.

Butler, Major General Smedley. Speech, 1933. Retrieved May 30, 2023. https://man.fas.org/smedley.htm

Colby, Jason. "'Banana Growing and Negro Management': Race, Labor and Jim Crow Colonialism in Guatemala, 1884-1930." Diplomatic History 30 (4),

September 2008. 595-621. JSTOR access May 27, 2023.

Daley, Mercedes. "The Watermelon Riot: Cultural Encounters in Panama City, April 15, 1856." Hispanic American Historical Review 70 (1), 1990. Retrieved May 31, 2023. https://read.dukeupress.edu/hahr/article/70/1/85/146726/The-Watermelon-Riot-Cultural-Encounters-in-Panama

Folse, Mark. "Never Known a Day of Peace." Naval History Magazine 35 (4), August 2021. Retrieved May 29, 2023. https://www.usni.org/magazines/naval-history-magazine/2021/august/never-known-day-peace

Han, Danielle. "Fruit Geopolitics: America's Banana Republics." JSTOR Daily, April 9, 1923. Accessed May 29, 2023. https://daily.jstor.org/fruit-geopeelitics-americas-banana-republics/

Haggerty, Richard. Haiti, A Country Study. Washington, D.C.: Library of Congress, 1989. Retrieved May 31, 2023. https://countrystudies.us/haiti/

Haggerty, Richard. The Dominican Republic, A Country Study. Washington D.C., Library of Congress, 1989. Retrieved May 31, 2023. https://countrystudies.us/dominican-republic/

Halton, Phil. Military History Now. "The Banana Wars—10 Quick Facts About America's Military Interventions in the Caribbean and Latin America." Retrieved May 30, 2023. https://militaryhistorynow.com/2020/09/20/the-banana-wars-10-quick-facts-about-americas-early-military-interventions-in-the-caribbean-latin-america/

Jansen, Kees. "Banana Wars and the Multiplicity of Conflicts in Commodity Chains." European Review of American and Caribbean Studies, 81. October 2006. Retrieved May 30, 2023. https://www.researchgate.net/publication/40111781_Banana_Wars_and_the_Multiplicity_of_Conflicts_in_Commodity_Chains

Jefferson, Mark. "Population Estimates for the Countries of the World 1914-1920." Bulletin of the American Geographical Society 46 (6) 1914. 401-13. JSTOR access Retrieved June 1, 2023.

Jewett, Philip. Latin American Wars 1900-41. New York: Bloomsbury Osprey, 2018.

Kohout, Mark. "Huerta, Victoriano." Texas State Historical Society. Retrieved June 3, 2023. https://www.tshaonline.org/handbook/entries/huerta-victoriano

Langley, Lester. The Banana Wars: United States Interventions in the Caribbean 1898-1934. Wilmington, Delaware: Scholarly Resources, 2002.

Meditz, Sandra, and Hanratty, Dennis. Panama, A Country Study. Washington, D.C.: Library of Congress, 1987. Retrieved June 5, 2023. https://countrystudies.us/panama/

Merrill, Tim. Honduras, A Country Study. Washington, D.C.: Library of Congress, 1995. Retrieved May 31, 2023. https://countrystudies.us/honduras/

Merrill, Tim. Nicaragua, A Country Study. Washington, D.C.: Library of Congress, 1989. Retrieved May 31, 2023. https://countrystudies.us/nicaragua/

Military History. "United States Occupation of Haiti." Retrieved May 31, 2023. https://military-history.fandom.com/wiki/United_States_occupation_of_Haiti

Naval History and Heritage Command. "The Occupation of Veracruz, Mexico. 1914." Retrieved May 31, 2023. https://www.history.navy.mil/browse-by-topic/wars-conflicts-and-operations/early-20th-century-conflicts/veracruz-1914.html

Peace History. United States Foreign Policy History and Resource Guide. "Yankee Imperialism 1901-1934." Retrieved June 6, 2023. http://peacehistory-usfp.org/yankee-imperialism/

Piatti-Farnell, Lorna. Bananas, A Global History. London: Reaktion Books, 2016.

Veggeberg, Vernon. A Comprehensive Approach to Counterinsurgency: The US Occupation of the Dominican Republic, 1916-1924. Thesis, United States Marine Corps. Quantico, VA, 2008. Retrieved May 30, 2023. https://apps.dtic.mil/sti/pdfs/ADA491390.pdf